Bhakti Sutras

of Narada

The Spiritual Path of Endless Love

Ethan Walker III

This book is dedicated to the lovers of the Divine and all those who would like to love the Divine and to the Divine Itself who pours back upon His/Her lovers an endless waterfall of grace, love and bliss

As long as you live in the mind,

you will continue to be bored. - Amma

BHAKTI SUTRAS OF NARADA

The Spiritual Path of Endless Love

Ethan Walker III

© Copyright 2016 by Devi Press, Inc.

Address all enquiries to:
Devi Press
PO Box 1605
Noble, OK 73068
info@devipress.com

First edition – First printing – May, 2016
Printed in the United States

ISBN 978-0-9729317-7-9

Contents

INTRODUCTION

Narada was a great sage who appears frequently and prominently in the ancient spiritual texts of India. The story goes that when the Creator made the universe, he also simultaneously created a number of beings who would be eternally enlightened. It would be their task to serve the rest of us by showing us the path to the Divine. Narada is one of these eternally free souls. He is a master musician and is often shown holding or playing a Veena which is a classical Indian stringed instrument. He appears throughout the epics such as the *Ramayana* and the *Mahabharata*. His favorite activity is singing devotional songs to the Lord and it is said his spirit is present when others sing to God with devotion. He is known for being a cosmic traveler going far and wide from the earth to celestial realms.

Writing the *Bhakti Sutras* is a fulfillment of Narada's mission to help and serve humanity. These sutras, any sutras, are a collection of short phrases each designed to express the essence of a topic and are like the flowers of a garland strung together on a common thread. In this case, the topic is love for God expressed in 84 sutras.

Bhakti is a Sanskrit word which literally means attachment, devotion, and love to or for God. Narada explains simply and powerfully how to merge in the Divine through the path of love and devotion.

The path of Bhakti, can be practiced by persons of any faith. Jesus said he had two commandments for us to follow:

> One of them, an expert in the law, tested him with this question: "Teacher, which is the greatest commandment in the Law?" Jesus replied: " 'Love the Lord your God with all your heart and with all your soul and with all your mind.' This is the first and greatest commandment. And the second is like it: 'Love your neighbor as yourself.' All the Law and the Prophets hang on these two commandments."
> *Matthew* 22:35-40, NIV

In the first commandment, Jesus asks us to take up the path of Bhakti. He says this is his first and greatest commandment. Jesus was a bhakta or a person who teaches or follows the path of love and devotion for the Beloved.

Bhakti is one of two paths to salvation. The other is the path of jnana or knowledge. In this case "knowledge" is like the Greek word *gnosis* which means a direct, intuitive knowing. Jnanis dive deeply into the source of their own awareness - the Self – the I AM THAT I AM. The God of bhaktas and the Self of jnanis are the same in the end. Both reside within us.

> And when he was demanded of the Pharisees, when the kingdom of God should come, he answered them and said, The kingdom of God cometh not with observation: Neither shall they say, Lo here! or,

lo there! for, behold, the kingdom of God is within you. *Luke* 17:20-21, KJV

When the Supreme is realized within, it is then experienced as being the entire universe with all distinction between inner and outer having been completely evaporated.

There are many reasons why one might want to read and contemplate the *Bhakti Sutras* of Narada. At the core of all these reasons, we are searching for happiness or contentment. There is nothing more satisfying than love. Love and love alone gives life meaning and beauty. Without love we are lost.

Everyone is capable of love and so it is the easiest, fastest and most enjoyable path to the Divine. Even if one does not become an enlightened saint in the foreseeable future, practicing bhakti is still worth the effort even if we only get small packets of bliss every now and then. The slightest whiff of love for the Divine is intoxicating beyond measure. Nothing can compare with the sweetness of devotion. Amma comments on this by comparing the path of jnana (knowledge) with the path of devotion. She uses the word *"mukti"* to represent the path of jnana. Those who pursue this path covet their pending liberation (mukti) from the confines of the illusory ego.

> Mother showed the tip of one of Her fingers. "In front of bhakti (devotion for God), mukti (liberation from the cycle of birth and death) is no more than this." Amma, *Eternal Wisdom*, book 2, page 194

3

A bhakta (one who practices devotion to God) is not primarily interested in liberation or salvation but only that he or she continues to love the Lord with all their heart, mind and soul. It is to this end that Narada has given us these beautiful *Bhakti Sutras*. If contemplated deeply, the reader will discover many buried treasures.

The author of the book you are holding in your hands began with Swami Vivekananda's translation of the *Bhakti Sutras* as a base camp. This was compared with several other translations. In addition, a word-for-word study was made of the Sanskrit transliterations. From these was derived the translation in this book. Swamiji's original text is 95% intact. In only a few instances did it seem to deviate from the Sanskrit enough to merit minor modifications.

The sutras are presented twice. The first round being a straight through read with no commentary. At times it is nice to simply read them without clutter so one can experience the power and beauty in the flowing river of the sutras. The sutras are then written a second time with commentary so that one can bring gold pans, tents, lawn chairs, picks and shovels and enjoy time rummaging in the streams, forests and fields of Divine Love.

THE BELOVED

The breath of the Beloved
Is a paintbrush in the hand of my heart
Always rearranging
The table where love sits
Calling like the open space
Of a pure white canvas
Calls to the paint
Take me; take it all
Love is the binding rope
That sets us free at last

Practicing devotion requires that we have a Beloved. That is, God in a personal form that is capable of receiving our devotion. A Beloved that is aware of our efforts and gives love, grace and compassion back to us as a willful act.

Many people have difficulty accepting that there is such a God. Some are able to go so far as to accept an underlying energy or the endless space of awareness, but to say that it is an organized and intelligent energy capable of personal communication is out of reach. This is regrettable but certainly understandable. The author was once an atheist and the story of his metamorphosis can be read in the autobiographical book *Into the Mystic* which is available at www.devipress.com.

Especially in western cultures, the intellect is regarded as the highest good. We think the intellect is our ticket to not only survival but a comfortable life. It buys food, pays the bills, invents new drugs and puts men on the moon. In this sense, the intellect is a wonderful computer. However, it is quite blind and incapable of any creative genesis. It is not capable of providing happiness and, in fact, when it is allowed to steer our ship, yields mostly suffering. For happiness – true lasting happiness – the heart must be in command of our ship. By "heart" we do not mean mere emotion but rather the core of our being which radiates light, love and bliss.

In our journey from infant to adult, the heart is ignored and it remains undeveloped; we have no sense of it – no connection or awareness of it. We are taught to do math and diagram sentences but nobody teaches us how to feel the sublime and subtle inner worlds of Being. For most of us the heart is the unwanted child that we keep locked in the dark space underneath the stairs. This is unfortunate because it is only through the heart that we may come face to face with God and dwell in the light of Supreme Love. God must first be felt in order to be seen.

Recent scientific research has demonstrated that the heart neuro-complex in the center of the chest is more cognizant than the brain with the heart sending far more information to the brain than the brain sends to the heart (www.heartmath.com).

> "There is a light that shines beyond the world, beyond everything, beyond all, beyond the highest heaven. This is the light that shines within your heart." – Upanishads

We have a cosmic wire, more like a spoke from a hub, that comes from the universe that is plugged in at the point of the heart in the center of the chest. It is through this portal that we access God and God communicates with us. The spoke comes up from the center of being and not through time and space. At the very center, we are all connected – everything is one being. At the center of being is The Beloved radiating out into all that exists for all eternity. This is the mechanism of devotion.

In Hindu yogic texts, the heart is regarded as being the seat of the soul. In the system of Jewish mysticism known as Kabbalah, the center of the Tree of Life is associated with the place of the heart. The Islamic mystics, the Sufis, have the concept of *Sirr* and describe it as the secret innermost heart of hearts where Allah reveals His mystery to Himself. In Catholicism, we have the concept of the Sacred Heart.

If we lack faith in a Beloved that is more than formless energy, we can somewhat reason our way to the portal of faith. It goes like this:

The entire sum of existence is a conscious, living being with a cosmic mind. We are made in the image of that or we could say we are a reflection of that. The universe is the body of God. At the core of being, and in the center of our own hearts, God is the eternal sun of consciousness (formless) which harbors light, life and love (form) for eternity. Thus every human, animal, plant, stone and atom has its existence in this flow of primordial energy and information.

7

The Hindu Vedas state that everything in the universe is ripples and waves appearing on the ocean of consciousness. If we can accept this to be a plausible explanation, then we can accept that something is alive, call it a cosmic mind, that is continually creating and destroying all forms of matter and energy. This is done willfully and with intelligence the same as if one would write a symphony and then conduct the playing of it.

This willful intelligence is evident if we examine Nature closely. The detail of circumstances in the human body alone, that allow legions of cells to live and work at different tasks, is mind numbing. And this is only one tiny speck. There is cohesion and harmony in atoms, molecules, weather, the solar system and in the functioning of the sun and galaxies. Everywhere we look we see incredible and vast details that dovetail perfectly. Even a single cell in a blade of grass is astonishingly complex. To think this all occurred by accident or by chance is more incredible and incomprehensible than to believe a mind was behind it all. In fact, the design we see and the interconnectedness of it all *is* mind! Only a person who has never studied Nature would assign the design to the trash bin of random chance. And it's not static – it's all moving! Why does it not all collide and collapse? What is directing and orchestrating this constant movement?

> "I see the Lord in His universe," the Master said, "Viewing a beautiful tree, my heart is moved and whispers: 'He is there!' I bow to adore Him. Doesn't

He permeate every atom of the earth? Could our planet exist at all except by the cohesive power of God? When we see Him in all persons, in all things; each rock becomes an altar.

Paramahamsa Yogananda

Beyond the design, where did all this come from? It could not come from nothing. Zero plus zero or zero times zero is always zero. We might consider that form (the design of matter and energy that is the universe) is eternally existing. Thus the universe was never created because it always has been. The Hindu Vedas describe a process of birth and death for the universe. When the universe is dissolved in the cosmic dissolution, another one is born. It expands and then begins to contract until it too dissolves and yet another universe is born. This has been occurring for eternity and will never cease. Thus there was no original creation.

Adi Shankara, (circa 800 CE) states in his treatise *The Crest Jewel of Discrimination*, that the universe (as form – as matter and energy) is eternal. While being credited with being the father of modern non-dual (jnana) philosophy, he was also a bhakta and worshiped God in the form of the Divine Mother. From this way of looking, the universe was never created – it always has been. The universe is the body of God and it is designed and orchestrated by this cosmic mind.

This same cosmic mind that is God, is capable of communicating with each of us on a very personal level. God is continuously communicating so much information to us now from the center of being and up through the heart. Every cell in our body contains all the genes necessary to be any type of cell. To be a liver cell, certain genes step to the front of the stage and bone cell genes recede into a dormant state. Modern science is baffled as to how each cell knows what to become. The answer is that God is continuously communicating with every cell. As previously stated, this communication comes from within us, from the core of all being, and manifests through the portal of the heart. The entire universe is centrally managed. Every atom, every particle floats in this stream of life that comes from within and does not have to travel through time and space. This communication is instantaneous. In this way, God can and will talk to us, love us and care for us. To say that this is not possible is to limit the limitless.

To practice devotion, it is most desirable to pick a form. God will appear to us in whatever form we are most drawn to. This could also be a physical incarnation of God such as Jesus, Amma or Krishna or one's guru provided the guru is a satguru - one who has merged permanently in the Divine.

Not only is the nature of God love, but God *is* love.

God is love. *1 John 4:8 and 4:16*

Where there is love, there Bhagavan (God) is. Amma, *Awaken Children*, vol. 1

If you focus your mind on me and revere me with all your heart, you will surely come to me; this I promise, because I love you. Krishna, *Bhagavad Gita*, 18:65

The path of love and devotion is the easiest, safest and most expedient path to the Divine.

The fact that the entire universe is alive as a singular living, loving intelligent being - a Divine Intelligence, a Divine Person if you will - that can and will communicate with us and that the very nature of this Divine Person is love, can be borne out by direct experience. One must proceed on faith at first but God will come if we call Him with love and longing. He must – it's His nature!

Constant remembrance of God, irrespective of time and place, is real devotion. If you practice in this manner, He will come; He must come. God will come and play with you. Amma, *Awaken Children*, vol. 3

The author would like to express his eternal gratitude to his guru Mata Amritanandamayi (Amma) without whom this book would never have been written because the author would still be groveling in the minutia of a meaningless existence.

The following poem, *A Golden Compass*, is from the 14th century Sufi poet Hafiz from *I Heard God Laughing – Readings of Hafiz*, translated by Daniel Ladinsky, Sufism Reoriented

A GOLDEN COMPASS

Forget every idea of right and wrong
   any classroom ever taught you
Because an empty heart, a tormented mind, unkindness,
   jealousy and fear
Are always the testimony
   you have been completely fooled!
Turn your back on those
   who would imprison your wondrous spirit
With deceit and lies.
Come, join the honest company of the King's beggars -
Those gamblers, scoundrels and divine clowns
   and those astonishing fair courtesans
Who need Divine Love every night.
Come, join the courageous who have no choice
   but to bet their entire world
That indeed, indeed, God is real.
I will lead you into the circle
   of the Beloved's cunning thieves,
Those playful royal rogues, the ones you can trust
   for true guidance -
Who can aid you in this blessed calamity of life.
Hafiz, look at the Perfect One at the circle's center:
He spins and whirls like a Golden Compass,
   beyond all that is rational,

To show this dear world
    that everything, everything in existence
Does point to God.

BHAKTI SUTRAS OF NARADA

1. Now in a spirit of auspiciousness, we will begin to reveal the path of bhakti or devotion to the Beloved.

2. Bhakti is a deep and consuming love for God.

3. It's very nature is the nectar of immortality.

4. Upon becoming immersed in devotion for the Beloved, one is made perfect, immortal and in possession of endless contentment.

5. In the fire of devotion all desires are brought to an end along with grief, aversions, rejoicing over fleeting pleasures and concern for one's personal self.

6. Becoming intoxicated with Divine Love, such a one is completely overwhelmed with the ecstasy of union and rejoices in the bliss of the infinite Self.

7. Spiritual devotion is not the child of desire. Its nature is the profound peace of renunciation.

8. Yet, it is this profound peace that gives guidance and meaning to spiritual observances and worldly actions. It is the ever fertile soil in which the lotus of compassion blooms.

9. Attaining this sublime devotion requires training the heart and mind to be one-pointed; looking always at the

Beloved with a heart filled with love and ignoring all that would distract from the goal.

10. Abandoning the illusory dwellings of the mind, one takes refuge in God alone.

11. Abandoning what is opposed to cultivation of love for the Beloved means worldly and traditional activities must be compatible with spiritual devotion.

12. Even after the development of spiritual devotion, there should be steadfast commitment to practicing the wisdom of the scriptures.

13. Or else there is danger of doing evil in the name of liberty.

14. When Divine Love is thoroughly rooted one may give up social forms but the body should be preserved by eating, drinking and wearing protective clothing.

15. Due to differences in point of view, various descriptions of spiritual devotion have been offered.

16. Sage Vyasa says a deep and forceful longing to perform ritual worship and ceremonial offerings is the expression of spiritual devotion.

17. According to Sage Garga, delighting in stories of the Beloved and engaging in discussions about the Lord is the hallmark of spiritual devotion.

18. And Sage Sandilya recounts that constantly feeling the bliss of the innermost Self is spiritual devotion.

19. However, Narada (the author) feels that spiritual devotion is the feeling that one is constantly offering every thought, word and deed to the Lord and feeling deep anguish at the least forgetfulness of his Beloved.

20. There have been numerous occurrences of this most sublime devotion.

21. The Gopis of Vrindavan had it.

22. Even at the highest pinnacle of devotion, one should stay fixed on the glory of the Beloved and not fall to pride which would extinguish the conduit of love.

23. Love which fails to bow to the glory of the Beloved is no more than the self-cherishing love of an unchaste person for his or her paramour.

24. In selfish love, there is no concern for the happiness of the paramour.

25. Devotion for the Beloved (bhakti yoga) is greater than the yogas of service (karma yoga), knowledge (jnana yoga) and traditional raja yoga.

26. Devotion is greater because the bliss of devotion is itself the fruit and is available from the beginning of the path. Pure, selfless love and devotion are the eventual goal of all other paths.

27. Love for the Beloved is also highest because the Lord cherishes humility and runs away from egotism.

28. Some say spiritual devotion is attainable through the path of knowledge of the Beloved.

29. Some say devotion and knowledge are both necessary.

30. Narada, the son of Brahma, says love for the Beloved is its own reward.

31. We can observe this in the examples of a king, a home, food and so on.

32. Knowledge does not make one royalty, satisfy one or remove hunger.

33. Therefore, the path of devotion alone is suitable for those who long to be free.

34. Great teachers have shown the path of devotion for the Beloved.

35. To develop love for the Beloved, it is vital to abandon fascination for and attachment to the myriad of objects that come and go in the five senses.

36. And by immersing oneself in unceasing adoration of the Beloved.

37. Love for God will come like a consuming fire while living in the world, listening to stories of the Beloved or singing the Lord's praises.

38. But mainly by the grace of God-realized Mahatmas and by a drop of the Lord's mercy.

39. However, these great Mahatmas are very rare and so their company is difficult to find. We cannot fathom their being and their presence is infallible.

40. Only by God's grace is one able to sit in the physical presence of such a one.

41. Because there is no difference between the grace of God and the grace of these Mahatmas.

42. Try to get the grace of God alone! Try to get the grace of God alone!

43. Abandon the company of worldly seeking persons as one would shun poison.

44. Because evil company is the cause of infatuation with pleasure, anger, forgetting spiritual goals, being unable to know right from wrong and the real from the unreal, and complete destruction.

45. At first, evil appears as ripples and then waves and soon swells into an all-consuming ocean in which one will surely drown.

46. Who can cross this ocean? Who can cross over this illusion of Maya? Only those who let go of bad company, who keep the company of the Saints and Sages and who are free from the feeling of "I" and "mine."

47. One who seeks solitude, serves the Great Ones, who eliminates desire and fear which are the chains of the world, who is no longer affected by the three qualities of nature, and who abandons the idea that happiness is dependent on things outside of oneself.

48. He who abandons expectation for the fruit or reward of one's activities, and is free from the pairs of opposites such as joy and sorrow, gain and loss and pain and pleasure.

49. And renouncing even the scriptures one is able to feel unbroken love for God.

50. Verily one crosses; he crosses this ocean of limitation and helps all the world to cross over.

51. The essential nature of this love between the lover and the Beloved can never be put into words or thoughts.

52. Like a person who is mute cannot describe what he tastes.

53. In some rare persons, this divine love is expressed with great brilliance like the sun radiates heat and light.

54. This love is felt as an exquisitely subtle and sublime bliss beyond the conditions of Nature, desireless, boundless and expanding moment by moment into the infinite.

55. Abiding in that fiery love for the Beloved, one sees love everywhere, hears love everywhere, speaks only of his Beloved and thinks of his Beloved alone.

56. There are three types of secondary devotion and, according to the qualities or conditions of each person, this love manifests itself differently.

57. Each succeeding type of devotion is more noble than the one before it.

58. The path of devotion is the simplest most direct way to salvation.

59. The proof of this is self-evident requiring no other proof.

60. Because its nature is peace and perfect bliss.

61. There is no anxiety because everything has been surrendered to the Lord.

62. Until devotion ripens, one should continue social customs and ceremonies with only the fruits of these activities relinquished.

63. Stories about sex, riches and the travails of worldly people should be avoided.

64. Egoism, pride and other negative mental afflictions should be abandoned.

65. If these passions cannot be controlled, direct them to God – place all your actions on God.

66. Going beyond the three forms (tamas, rajas, sattva) of devotion, the devotee sees himself as God's eternal servant or eternal bride and one's only reason for existence is to love.

67. Devotees who have given themselves solely to God are the highest.

68. When such speak of God, their voices stick in their throats, they cry and weep, their hairs stand on end; and it is they who give holy places their holiness; they make good works, good books better, because they are permeated with God.

69. They add holiness to holy places, nobleness to acts and they elevate mere writings to the level of sacred scriptures.

70. They are given the fullness of God to know the presence of the Beloved in and around themselves at all times.

71. When a man loves God so much, his forefathers rejoice, the gods dance, and the earth gets a Master!

72. To such lovers there is no difference of caste, sex, knowledge, form, birth, or wealth

73. For they all belong to God.

74. Logic and intellectual grasping are to be avoided.

75. Because these can never fathom the unfathomable, they continue endlessly and to no good end.

76. One should read books that are flush with devotion and one should do practices that increase it.

77. Giving up all desires of pleasure and pain, gain and loss, worship God day and night. Not a moment is to be spent in vain.

78. Ahimsâ (non-violence), truthfulness, purity, compassion, and godliness are always to be kept.

79. The Lord alone should be worshipped at all times, with all one's heart and soul, and with a calm mind.

80. Giving up all other thoughts, the whole mind should day and night worship God. Thus being worshipped day and night, He reveals Himself and makes His worshippers feel Him.

81. In all of the past, present and future, love alone is the highest reality!

82. Though devotion itself is a singularity, it manifests in eleven basic modes.

Contemplating the greatness of God
Cherishing God's beauty and form
Loving to worship God
Remembering God at all times
Being the servant of God
Being the friend of God
Being an affectionate parent to God
Being married to God
Dedication to God
Becoming absorbed in God
Permanent self-obliteration in God

83. Thus the luminaries of the path of devotion - Sanatkumara, Vyasa, Suka, Sandilya, Garga, Vishnu, Kaundinya, Sesha, Uddhava, Aaruni, Bali, Hanuman, Vibhishana and others-proclaim unanimously without fear of the criticism of men.

84. Those who believe and have faith in this auspicious teaching given by Narada, become blessed with devotion and will realize the Beloved and attain the Beloved.

SUTRAS WITH COMMENTARY

Sutra 1 – Narada begins to reveal the path

Now in a spirit of auspiciousness, we will begin to reveal the path of bhakti or devotion to the Beloved.

athato bhaktim vyakhyasyamah

atha-now; *atah*-therefore; *bhaktim*-bhakti (devotion for God); *vyakhyasyamah*-we shall explain

Conscious, focused awareness narrows into a concentrated point causing the eternal Now to bloom with great effulgence filling the lover of the Divine or soon-to-be lover of the Divine with a sense of anticipation. It flows like a current through the nervous system producing a blissful sort of energy but it is inward reaching and of an eternal nature as opposed to the sort of excitement one might feel toward fleeting worldly objects.

This auspicious feeling is the Beloved playing through the body's energy channels beckoning and urging the lover to take a step. Calling with such great love and affection, the Beloved waits with open arms to receive His/Her prodigal daughter or son.

Narada, beaming with great joy, is poised to reveal the path. He was created for this purpose and nothing else will fill him with so much bliss. He anticipates showing us the path as much as we anticipate his guidance. In this dance, we are already bonding with Narada and love begins to flow between him and us. It is as though we are a missing piece of Narada and he is a missing piece of our own destiny. We feel that we know him. We are cut from the same cloth of bhakti (devotion). Narada is a part of us and we are a part of him.

ALL THAT IS CERTAIN

Eternal Mother
Fishermen know the secret
They bait their hook with love and wait

A candle knows too
It lets itself be consumed
So it can rise to heaven

Mother what do you have to show us
In the scattered foray
Of these minds that pine for peace?
Is this your doing
Or is this the curious effort of your children?

Mother you are all that is certain
When the curtains are closed
And the crowd is gone
And the lonely gaslight
Hisses beneath the starry sky
On the corner of Bliss Street and Love

[From the author's book *Divine Mother of the Universe*]

Sutra 2 – A consuming love for God

Bhakti is a deep and consuming love for God.

sa tvasmin parama-prema-rupa

sa–it (bhakti); *tvasmin*–for the Beloved; *parama*-greatest; *prema*-selfless love; *rupa*-in the form of

We can only cry Oh! Oh! Oh! with fiery tears streaming down our cheeks as we are swept up into the arms of the Beloved! Bricks become dust as our wall of separation crumbles. The reunion is unimaginable. God rises from the deepest core of our being as infinite light, life and love. We experience God filling infinite space with the intelligent willing of all that exists. We are overwhelmed by the love that floods our being. We know beyond all doubt that He sees us and that He is loving us. God takes us in His arms and holds us so close. We put our arms around Her neck and whisper so softly, "I love you so much!" This love is beyond anything we had ever imagined and we are entirely uprooted by it. We are rushing helplessly and gratefully down a river of unstoppable bliss.

The deep and consuming love of bhakti is selfless. It has no thought of a return or a reward - even abandoning notions of liberation. This love exists only for its own sake. Selfish love is what most of us experience in the world. Swami Vivekananda called this "shopkeeper's love" in

27

which one gives love in order to get something. This is a lower order of love and not the same as bhakti.

Amma comments:

> Spiritual love is different. The beginning is beautiful and peaceful. Shortly after this peaceful beginning comes the agony of longing. Through the middle period, the agony will continue to grow stronger and stronger, more and more unbearable. Excruciating pain will ensue, and this pain of love will prevail until just before it leads up to unity with the beloved. This unity is beautiful, even more inexpressibly beautiful than the beginning of love. The beauty and peace of this unity in love remains forever and ever. Love of this kind never dries up or diminishes. Always alive, both within and without, it is constant, and each moment you live in love. Love will swallow you, eat you up completely until there is no 'you,' only Love. Your whole being will be transformed into Love. Spiritual love culminates in unity, in oneness. Amma, *Awaken Children*, vol. 4

Sutra 3 – It's nature is immortality

It's very nature is nothing less than immortality.

amrita-svarupa ca

amrita–immortal; *svarupa*–essence; *ca*-and

We live in a sea of moving, changing objects upon which our minds have been wholly fixed up until now. Reveling in the bliss of divine love, we experience this love as the changeless substratum of every experience. Love and awareness are the same. We realize that by God's grace we have stumbled upon the door to immortality. Tibetans consider this nectar of immortality (amrita) to be the ultimate medicine which cures the disease of Samsara which is the endless rounds of births and deaths that spiral around our personal polestar of separation. Drinking this nectar allows the lover to merge with the Beloved by shedding the limited ego.

> Be ye therefore perfect, even as your Father which is in heaven is perfect. Jesus, *Matthew* 5:48, KJV

Divine love is the antithesis of the ego. Where one is, the other will not remain. It is impossible for both to coexist at the same time. The ego is all about me... me... me... while divine love is all about Thee... Thee... Thee... When the ego or sense of separation is consumed in the blaze of bhakti, we become the immortal Beloved. Amma comments:

29

Having attained human form, we should elevate ourselves to the Divine. We should surrender our individual selves totally to God and thus become perfect. Amma, *Omkara Divya Porule*, part 6

DRAW ANOTHER CUP OF JOY

Compassionate Mother
 who's grace is the cradle of eternity
My friends and I will draw another cup of joy
 from the wellspring of your radiant heart

And raise it to our lips with a shout
 Victory to the Mother!
  Victory to the Mother of all beings!

And when this tavern of divine revelry
 closes in the morning's wee hours

We will all walk home arm in arm
 with faltering steps
 to our conventional minds
  staggering with the intoxication of love
   and waking the neighbors
    shouting like bugle blowers

Victory to the Mother!
Victory to the Mother of the universe!

[From the author's book *Soft Moon Shining*]

Sutra 4 – One is made perfect

Upon becoming immersed in devotion for the Beloved, one is made perfect, immortal and in possession of endless contentment.

yat labdhva puman siddho bhavaty amrto bhavaty trpto bhavaty

yat-which; *labdhva*-having gained; *puman*-a person; *siddha*-perfect; *bhavaty*-becomes; amṛtah–immortal; *bhavati*-becomes; *trypta*-fully content; *bhavati*-becomes

Love charms the mind like the flute player charms a cobra. Filled with love for the Divine, the mind now gazes into the glowing cauldron of blissful love, firmly fixed and one-pointed. The mind is quiet and peaceful warming itself in front of the potbellied stove of the heart while the winter storms of ignorance and depravity that rage just outside the door go completely unnoticed.

Pleasures of the past are dead and buried. They cannot compete with the Divine which fills the lover with the most exquisite bliss. Utterly void of distractions, the lover melts into ultimate contentment. Having been thus made perfect, there is no further goal as the highest has been reached.

Liberation or salvation is not something the lover pursued or even thought about. His mind and heart were given wholly to the Lord. Rather, liberation is given to the lover by the grace and compassion of the Beloved. Thus the desireless devotee becomes a siddha or perfected one.

31

Only by undistracted love can men see me, and know me, and enter into me. He who does my work, who loves me, who sees me as the highest, free from attachment to all things, and with love for all creation, he in truth comes to me. Krishna, *Bhagavad Gita* 11:54–55

The Sanskrit word *labdhva* (having gained; obtained) in this sutra is significant because it expresses the idea that anyone, regardless of gender, religion, race and so on, can develop devotion (bhakti) and attain salvation or liberation (mukti).

Whoever comes into the river of Love will be bathed in it, whether the person is healthy or diseased, a man or a woman, someone wealthy or someone poor. Anyone can take any number of dips in it. Amma, *Awaken Children* vol. 5

Sutra 5 – All desires end in devotion

In the fire of devotion all desires are brought to an end along with grief, aversions, rejoicing over fleeting pleasures and concern for one's personal self.

yat prapya na kincid vanchati na socati na dvsti na ramate notsahi bhavati

yat-which (bhakti-devotion); *prapya*-having attained; *na kinchit*-absence of; *vanchati*-desires; *na socati*-without regret, without lamenting; *na dvsti*-has no aversions; *na ramate*-does not rejoice in temporary happiness; *notsahi*-without interest in self-centered concerns; *bhavati*-becomes

Self-cherishing is the wholesale preoccupation with one's personal self. The afflictive emotions such as grief, hatred, anger, lust, pride, greed, fear and so on, grow and flourish in the fertile soil of our self-cherishing. Day by day this self-created tiny prison cell crumbles in the light of our love for God. The focus of our attention shifts from "what's in it for me" to "I love you so much!" The very root of our primal psychosis is removed thus causing the desires we once worshiped to vanish like mist in the morning sun.

Sri Ramakrishna comments on worldly attachment, desires and pleasures:

> Worldly people say that it is impossible to be free from attachment to worldliness. But when God is

33

attained, all worldly attachment vanishes. After realizing the absolute bliss of God-consciousness one cannot enjoy sense-pleasures or run after fame, honor or any worldly object. Moths, after once seeing the light, do not return to the darkness. As much as one thinks of God and meditates on Him, by so much will one lose one's taste for worldly pleasures. As much as one's love and devotion for God increases, by so much will diminish worldly desires and care for the body. Then one will look upon every woman as mother, upon his own wife as a spiritual helpmate; all animal passions will disappear; Divine spirituality will come, and non-attachment to the world; then one will become absolutely emancipated even in this life. *Gospel of Ramakrishna*, translated by Swami Abhedananda

Sutra 6 – Overwhelmed with ecstasy

Becoming intoxicated with Divine Love, such a one is completely overwhelmed with the ecstasy of union and rejoices in the bliss of the infinite Self.

yat jnatva matto bhavati stabdo bhavaty atma ramo bhavati

yat- with that (bhakti); *jnatva-*knowing, realizing; *mattah-*intoxicated; *bhavati-*becomes; *stabdah-*stunned, overwhelmed; *bhavati-*becomes; *atma-aramah-*rejoice in the Divine Self; *bhavati-*becomes

For this sutra we are providing first an explanation of intoxication with the Beloved and then two descriptions of events. The reader should be advised that ecstatic union with God does not have to be this dramatic. Amma says that if we simply get tears for God we are saved.

Paramahamsa Ramakrishna (1836-1886) was a great God-intoxicated saint who lived in Dakshineswar, India. In the *Gospel of Ramakrishna*, translated by Swami Abhedananda, the Master comments on the state of absorption in the Beloved:

> Every man has certain debts to pay — a debt to the Divine Spirit, a debt to the sages, debt to mother, to father, to the wife. No man can renounce everything without paying off these debts. But if his soul be intoxicated with Divine Love and become mad after God, then he is free from all duties and debts. Then who is his father, who is his mother and who is his

35

wife? He behaves like a madman who is free from all bondage and who has no duty to perform. Do you know what that madness of Divine Love is?

In that state one forgets the world and becomes unconscious of one's own body which is so dear to one. Chaitanya Deva possessed this madness of ecstasy. He had neither hunger, nor thirst, nor sleep, nor consciousness of his physical form. The meaning of the word Chaitanya is "indivisible and absolute intelligence." Vaishnava Charan used to say that Chaitanya Deva, the Incarnation of Divine Love, was like a bubble on the ocean of that Absolute Intelligence.

Divine Love is the rarest thing in the world. He who can love God as a devoted wife loves her husband, attains to Divine Love. Pure love is difficult to acquire. In pure love the whole heart and soul must be absorbed in God. Then will come ecstasy. In ecstasy a man remains dumb with wonder. Outward breathing stops entirely, but inward breathing continues: as when aiming a gun, a man remains speechless and without breathing. In Divine Love one entirely forgets the external world with all its charms and attractions; even one's own body, which is so dear to one, is easily forgotten.

In ecstasy, when the breathing stops, the whole mind remains absolutely fixed upon the Supreme. All nerve currents run upward with tremendous force and the result is Samadhi or God-consciousness. Those who are mere scholars (Pandits) and have not attained Divine Love, confound the minds of others.

Sri Ramakrishna describes the first time the Divine Mother (the form of God he worshiped) appeared to him. The Master had experienced brief periods of ecstasy which resulted in the loss of outer consciousness prior to the appearance of the Divine Mother. As a young man and a Kali temple priest, he had been forging a deep love for the Cosmic Feminine. His supplication, prayers and longing reached a peak.

> I felt as if my heart were being squeezed like a wet towel. I was overpowered with a great restlessness and a fear that it might not be my lot to realize Her (the Divine Mother) in this life. I could not bear the separation from Her any longer. Life seemed to be not worth living. Suddenly my glance fell on the sword that was kept in the Mother's temple.

> I determined to put an end to my life. When I jumped up like a madman and seized it, suddenly the blessed Mother revealed herself. The buildings with their different parts, the temple and everything else vanished from my sight, leaving no trace whatsoever, and in their stead I saw a limitless, infinite Ocean of Consciousness. Within me there was a steady flow of undiluted bliss. *The Gospel of Sri Ramakrishna,* translated by Swami Nikhilananda

The following is an account of Mata Amritanandamayi (Amma) going into a state of devotional ecstasy. In her early days (teens and twenties), Amma would go into these states frequently – almost daily. She was so absorbed in the Divine, she struggled to keep her awareness in the world.

At one point Balu was describing the Mahatma's intense longing to realize God. He was depicting the excruciating pain of separation from his beloved deity through the following song, *Kera Vrikshannale...*

O trees and creepers,
Have you seen my Mother?
O glittering stars,
Where has my Mother gone?
O birds of the night that sing in the trees,
Did my Mother pass this way?
O Lady Night,
Where can I find my Mother?

I am wandering along every shore,
crying and seeking my Mother.
O my Beloved Mother,
I will ask every particle of sand
To tell me where You are.

Hearing these verses and their description of the intense yearning and agony of separation, Amma entered into a deep state of Samadhi. At first She silently shed tears of bliss and then, suddenly, Amma burst into blissful laughter. After this had gone on for some time, in Her ecstasy, Amma began to roll very fast on the ground like a spinning wheel. As She rolled around, Amma continued to laugh. For some time, the brahmacharins (monks) watched in wonder and awe. But when after a few minutes Amma showed no sign of coming out of Her ecstatic mood, they began to worry. It was not the first time that they had seen Mother like this, and in the past, She Herself had instructed them to sing bhajans in order to coax Her back to the normal plane of consciousness should She remain in Samadhi for more than a short while. And so, gathering in a corner of Amma's small room, the five brahmacharis began quietly to sing *Nirvanashatkam* (*Manobuddhya*)...

I am not the mind, intellect, ego or memory,
I am not the taste of the tongue
Or the senses of hearing, smell and sight,
I am not earth, fire, water, air or ether.
I am Pure Bliss Consciousness.
I am Shiva.

I am not right or wrong actions,
Nor am I pleasure or pain.
I am not the mantra or any sacred places,
The Vedas or the sacrifice.
I am not the act of eating, the eater or the food.

I am Pure Bliss Consciousness.
I am Shiva.

I have no birth or death,
Nor have I any fear.
I don't hold any caste distinction.
I have not father or mother
Associates or friends.
I have no Guru
And I have no disciple.
I am Pure Bliss Consciousness.
I am Shiva.

I have no form
Or movements of the mind.
I am the all-pervasive.
I exist everywhere,
Yet I am beyond the senses.
I am not salvation
Or anything that may be known.
I am Pure Bliss Consciousness.
I am Shiva.

In Her God-intoxicated state, Amma continued to roll and laugh for ten or fifteen minutes. Finally, She got up from the floor and began moving around the room as if drunk. Amma stumbled about with faltering steps, laughing blissfully all the while. Her fingers were held in identical divine mudras, and Her face glowed, emitting a penetrating radiance. Several times Amma's head or body came close to hitting the walls or banging against the floor, but the brahmacharins were very watchful and protected Her from any possible harm. For some time, Amma remained in one spot and gently swayed from side to side, reveling in Her own world, a world to which no one else had access. Eventually Amma lay down on the floor and remained still. The brahmacharins continued to sing until Amma had finally descended from Her exalted state. Swami Amritaswarupananda, *Awaken Children*, vol. 7

Sri Ramakrishna also struggled at times to keep his mind out of the Cosmic and in the earthly plane. He would stamp his feet and beg the Divine Mother to keep him present so he could talk to those who were visiting him. Ramakrishna and Amma are beings of a very high spiritual magnitude who came to this earth with a spiritual mission. Amma also recounts her struggle to remain conscious in the world after being asked about her divine moods:

> Amma: (Abstractedly) Oh...I don't know. They just come like that. (After a short pause) Do you know how much I am struggling to stay here in this world in the midst of all of you? It is really very difficult. But when Mother remembers the sorrows and sufferings of the people, Her mind melts and becomes compassionate. That is what keeps Her mind down here. As told by Swami Amritaswarupananda, *Awaken Children*, vol. 2

Sutra 7 – Not the child of desire

Spiritual devotion is not the child of desire. Its nature is the profound peace of renunciation.

sa na kamayamana nirvodha-rupatvat

sa-that (bhakti); *na*-not; *kamayamana*-coming from desire; *nirvodha-rupatvat*-its form is renunciation

Desire is always about "me." Love is always about something other than me – in this case, love for God. The first is selfish by nature and the second is selfless by nature. Herein lies the fundamental difference and an understanding as to why love for God is not a desire in the worldly sense.

When the fire of love burns, it consumes the "I" and along with it notions of relationships whether with persons or objects. One becomes fully aware in the present moment.

In the beginning of the practice of bhakti, the lover will harbor an initial desire to merge in God, to behold God, to hug God. This dualistic desire is to be expected due to the fact that we begin our spiritual journey from our delusional frame of reference which is dual in nature. Not only is this desire to be expected but it is necessary. Without the desire for God or God-realization, we would never make any effort.

Our minds currently dwell in duality. I am an "I" and everything else is an "other" and the purpose of the

42

"other" is to support the illusion of the "I." All spiritual practices must begin in duality. Even the path of jnana (a.k.a. advaita, Vedanta, non-duality) begins in duality with an investigation into the source of the "I." There is the dualistic notion of that which is investigated and also the investigator.

To desire an ice cream cone and to satisfy that desire leaves in its wake the desire for yet another ice cream cone. Of course it is not possible to be continuously eating ice cream and the experience does not continue to satisfy. Before long we need something more robust to titillate our need for pleasure. What results is an endless escalation which ends in exhaustion and frustration.

To desire the Beloved has the opposite effect. Our need to experience pleasure from things of the world diminishes as we begin to experience the bliss and love that flows between us and God. There was never a time that this love was not there but we were not aware of it simply because our awareness was so dim. Spiritual practices such as increasing our love and devotion increases this awareness.

With regards to the sense of "I," the practice of devotion for the Beloved is like the snake eating its tail. The desire for God is the one desire that brings an end to all desires. It is a secret trap door in the mind from which one can escape Samsara (endless rounds of births and deaths shadowed by continuous suffering).

43

In the following quote, Amma has been asked about the difference between worldly desires and the desire for God. She comments that worldly desires are futile and dissipate one's energy and then contrasts that with the desire for the Beloved:

> But with a spiritual seeker it is not so. His one and only desire is to realize God. He does everything with that as his goal. He has no worldly desires to fulfill. He withdraws his senses from worldly objects and fixes them on the form of his Beloved Deity. He sees that form in whatever he beholds. He tries to do everything selflessly. Therefore, there is no dissipation of energy. All desires end in his desire for God. His desire is for the highest and if that desire is fulfilled, he can save thousands from the cycle of rebirth. He becomes like a tree giving shade and fruit to all humanity. He gives peace and tranquility to any person who approaches him.
> Amma, *Awaken Children*, vol. 2

It is a common mistake to think that love is an emotion. In truth, it is much deeper than thoughts and emotions. Love is the subtle tether of unity in the world of the many. Every person and object in this universe swims in an ocean of love.

Singularity and renunciation are two words that are closely related. Upon realizing singularity, renunciation of desires and fears will be the spontaneous result. If one practices renunciation, then singularity will be the result.

"Whoever it may be, without renunciation one cannot realize God." Amma, *Awaken Children*, vol. 1

So then every one of you! He who does not renounce all he has is not able to be a disciple of mine. Jesus, *Luke* 14:33

In a singularity, the notions of "me" and "other" have no meaning. Me and other are two things whereas a singularity is not two things. Therefore, in a singularity such as love, all else is necessarily renounced. That does not mean the world disappears but the distinction between ourselves and the world disappears bringing an end to desire and fear and this delivers the lover to the realm of profound peace - stillness.

Paramahamsa Ramakrishna describes the state of dispassion:

A devotee: Bhagavan, what condition of mind is necessary for a worldly person to attain to freedom?

Ramakrishna: If by the Grace of the Lord strong dispassion for worldly things arises in his mind, then such a person becomes free from all earthly attachment. What is this *strong* dispassion? Let me tell you. Ordinary dispassion makes the mind think of the Lord occasionally, but there is no longing in the heart. Strong dispassion, on the contrary, makes the mind dwell constantly on the Lord with the same intense longing as a mother feels for her only child. He who has strong dispassion does not want anything but the Lord. He looks at the world as a deep well and is always fearful lest he may fall into it. Earthly relations seem to him very distant. He does not seek their company. His whole heart and soul yearn for God. He does not think of his family, nor does he think of the morrow. He also possesses great spiritual force.   *Gospel of Ramakrishna,* translated by Swami Abhedananda

The topic of renunciation is further explored in the author's book *Rama's Most Excellent Dispassion – The Path to Bliss*. Also, the "how to" of practicing bhakti is illustrated in the author's book *Finding Gods Love – The Theory and Practice of Love and Devotion as a Spiritual Path*.   Go to www.devipress.com to explore or purchase these books.

Sutra 8 – Profound peace gives guidance

Yet, it is this profound peace that gives guidance and meaning to spiritual observances and worldly actions. It is the ever fertile soil in which the lotus of compassion blooms.

nirodhas tu loka-veda-vyapara-nyasah

nirodah-renunciation; *tu*-but (in context of previous sutra); *loka*-woldly customs; *veda*-and of scriptures; *vyapara*-as the result of; *nyasa*- renunciation

The Great Activity arises from silence – the peace that surpasses understanding. Awareness is another word for this silence. It is timeless and so it has no beginning or end and it is of the nature of infinitely vast space. It has no form yet all of existence depends on it. It is utterly still yet it is more than alive and is known as the I Am at the core of one's being. The mind sees and experiences the reflection of awareness in the objects of the five senses like looking in a mirror. One comes to know of oneself as this very same awareness by focusing the mind on it. Then it is felt or "known" clearly but never observed. The Vedas tell us that the entire universe is nothing more than ripples and waves appearing on the ocean of awareness. If it were not for awareness – empty, still, silent - nothing could exist. When the mind becomes this stillness, the dance of existence is perfect.

In this sutra, Narada comments that inner peace (awareness) is practical and utilitarian. It has tangible value because stillness allows creativity to bloom (the perfect dance of existence). All creativity percolates up from the heart - from the core of being - and when the mind is still, the voice of the heart can be expressed. From this, one receives inspiration and guidance providing solutions to problems thus revealing a harmonious path through the world.

Love is the all-pervading tether that holds the seemingly separate objects of the universe like an ocean holds fish. When stillness and profound peace reign, love becomes the soul's guiding light. When all is still, love is revealed. Compassion then, is love in action and, in the fertile soil of profound peace, compassion begins to act on the world. In this way human-kind begins to move away from chaos and depravity and toward the harmony of God. Love, insight, wisdom, compassion – all of these arise spontaneously from the Great Silence.

Amma comments on silence and love:

> The real connection is between love and silence. When there is real love, there is silence. There cannot be any words. There is only stillness. Just like a perfectly calm lake, there cannot be any ripples or waves when real love is experienced. Ripples and waves are a distortion, a distraction, a disturbance in the mental lake. Love ensues from stillness of mind. In that stillness one can experience silence.

The talking of the mind stops completely. Real love is felt in that silence. Silence, silence alone, is the language of pure love. Real love exists in the heart. The love that exists in the heart cannot be spoken; it cannot be put in words. The heart is not the place for words. Amma, *Awaken Children*, vol. 5

Sutra 9 – Training heart and mind

Attaining this sublime devotion requires training the heart and mind to be one-pointed; looking always at the Beloved with a heart filled with love and ignoring all that would distract from the goal.

tasminn ananyata tad-virodhisudasinata ca

tasminn-in that (sublime devotion); *ananyata*-single minded, whole-hearted; *tad-virodhis*-for those things which are opposed; *udasinata*-indifference (renunciation); *ca*-and

Progress with any spiritual path requires a one-pointed mind and heart. In our current state – beginners all of us – our minds are allowed to wander wherever they will go. We have not given any consideration to inspecting our thoughts, controlling thoughts or eliminating thoughts.

Narada is saying we must do two things with the mind. First, it must always be directed to the Beloved with love pouring out from our heart like a roaring river. The second item is that the mind must be kept out of the bars, pool halls and dens of iniquity (figuratively and literally speaking) that serve only to distract us and cause us not to have a single-pointed mind.

Needless to say this all requires effort – a lot of effort. Not to be dismayed, we can think of our effort in small parcels or bricks that we can lay one by one. Thinking this way, it will not seem overwhelming. One brick might be contemplating love for God for ten minutes each morning. Another brick might be saying our mantra as we drive the first ten blocks to our place of work. Rope off small parcels – small enough that we can be victorious every day. In time, these will increase naturally if we continue to practice consistently on a daily basis.

What can be distracting? Everything is distracting! This is the illusory power of Maya which convinces us of the importance of our favorite TV show. Maya drags us into a dreamlike state and convinces us that we don't need to do anything. It doesn't help that everyone we know is also mesmerized, hypnotized and hog-tied by this powerful dream.

Sri Ramakrishna talks about making the effort:

> A devotee: Bhagavan, how can one make acquaintance with the Landlord (God)?
>
> Râmakrishna: For that, I say, work is necessary. What is the use of sitting quietly and saying, "God exists"? If you merely sit on the shore of a lake and say: "There are fish in this lake," will you catch any? Go and get the things necessary for fishing, get a rod and line and bait and throw some lure in the water. Then from the deep water the fish will rise and come nearer, and you will be able to see and catch them. You wish me to show you God while you sit quietly by, without making the least effort. How unreasonable! You would have me set the curds,

churn the butter, and hold it before your mouths. You ask me to catch the fish and place it in your hands. How unreasonable! If a man desires to see the King in his palace, he will have to go to the palace and pass through all the gates; but if after entering the outermost gate he exclaims, "Where is the King?" he will not find him. He must go on through the seven gates, then he will see the King. *Gospel of Ramakrishna,* translated by Swami Abhedananda

Amma comments on one-pointedness:

Question: Mother, what should be done to get one-pointedness?

Amma: Children, you should make an attempt and see for yourself. Initially, it is difficult to get concentration. Don't stop your meditation and other spiritual practices because there is no concentration. Constant practice is the only way to achieve it. Until yesterday we were living in another world, the world of illusion (Maya). The experiences we had there will trouble us at first. Son, the samskaras (accumulated tendencies) of so many births are there in our mind. When we start doing sadhana (spiritual practice), we can see all the negativity coming out and getting exhausted, just as more and more dirt comes off when we wipe the floor using a wet cloth. The mind can be made peaceful by sitting in solitude. Son, concentration will not be attained in the beginning. It is absolutely necessary to have a strong resolve to reach the goal.

HIDING IN PLAIN SIGHT

Laughing Mother
How can a leaf
Enter a tree?
But a smile
Goes both ways
Like a radiant sun
It lights up the world
And warms the heart

Mother
There is no way
Of living apart from you
Why do so few see this?

You are hiding
In plain sight
But a fish has no idea
About water

[From the author's book *Divine Mother of the Universe*]

Sutra 10 – Refuge in God alone

Abandoning the illusory dwellings of the mind, one takes refuge in God alone.

anyasrayanam tyago nanyata

anya-other; *asrayanam*-shelter, refuge; *tyagah*-abandoning; *an-anyata*-single-heartedly

In the mind are many mansions. All of them are the product of dreaming and built wholly with dream-stuff. We project these onto the world creating our own quasi-reality as we walk unconsciously through life. We cling to these illusory mansions with unwarranted tenacity. Abandoning any of them evokes a deep sense of fear and insecurity due to the fact that our illusory ego defines itself by identifying with these self-created realities. For example, we may harbor the idea that we are of a certain political persuasion. This is a mansion that we create in our minds and then decorate the interior with a myriad of ideologies and opinions. Our ego identifies with it – we say to ourselves and others, "I am a Republicrat!" We feel strongly that we are that. This is an example of a dwelling we create in the mind that becomes a place of refuge – a place of refuge for the ego. In our mind we have created so many of these – gender, race, religion, food preferences, petty annoyances – the list is vast.

> The burden and constant noise of your mind is a heavy load to carry. It has become an enormous

load, enough to overwhelm you. The pitiful thing about this is that you who are carrying this load are not aware of its terrible weight. - Amma, *Awaken Children*, vol. 6

There is nothing good about the mind. This statement does not mean that we should forget how to read or do arithmetic or solve a construction problem. These are like using a computer. What is not good about the mind is our propensity to constantly live in the past and the future, projecting our invented interpretations onto events that occur in our lives sucking us ever deeper into the maelstrom of our desires and fears. This is hell. Rather, the mind should be a computer that we access when we need to add our monthly budget numbers and then it should be put away until it's needed again. The rest of it – past, future, projecting our fantasies – this is killing us.

> People point their finger at insane people and call them 'crazy.' But they don't know that they themselves are actually crazy, as well. Whoever has a mind is mad, because the mind is madness. In the case of a person who is insane, it is clearly manifested and therefore you can see it. Whereas, in your case, it is not so clearly manifested and therefore not as obvious. But the madness is there, because the mind is there. - Amma, *Awaken Children*, vol. 6

We live in this madness which means we have taken refuge in a prison of sorrow while Narada is saying get out of all that and take refuge in God alone. In addition, these "illusory dwellings" are our main source of distraction. They will prevent us from developing a head of steam sufficient to propel us down the spiritual track. They will leak out all of our spiritual energy dooming us to be chained to our couch of mortality sucking our thumb in front of the television.

Sutra 11 – Activities must be compatible

Abandoning what is opposed to cultivation of love for the Beloved means worldly and traditional activities must be compatible with spiritual devotion.

loka-vedesu tad-anukulacaranath tad-virodhisudasinata

loka — in society; *vedesu*-and in sacred activities; *tad-anukulacaranath*-actions which nourish bhakti (devotion for the Divine); *tad-virodhisu*-opposed to bhakti; *udasinata*-disinterest

This sutra is reminiscent of Buddha's *Eight-fold Path* which is the following: Right view, intention, speech, action, livelihood, effort, mindfulness and concentration. The way in which we conduct our lives should be brought into harmony with the fulfillment of our goal.

Right view is to know that we are caught in Samsara which is the seemingly endless rounds of births and deaths accompanied by the ever present shadow of suffering. The suffering is the conditioned, limited existence in which it is perceived that we are separate from God, each other and the universe. We see that the practice of love for the Beloved is a way to transcend this ageless mortal grind. However, the world sees through different eyes. It is not only content in its suffering but will defend the causes of this suffering and will resist any attempt by others to go beyond. Therefore, one must work diligently to maintain the right view.

> People have a hard time letting go of their suffering. Out of a fear of the unknown, they prefer suffering that is. - Thich Naht Hahn

Our intention is to practice devotion. From the time we are born the world is telling us a different story. We are told that happiness lies not in love and devotion but in success with the activities of the world. Go to school, get married, get a good job, buy a house and a boat – and then we will be happy. Having discovered the fallacy in this, and/or having perceived the bliss of the Divine, we are intent on going to God on a boat of love and devotion.

Our speech should reflect the truth that our Beloved is embodied in every aspect of the world from the least to the greatest. Our words must be fitted with a bridle and saddle and subjected to constant scrutiny. Uttering a word of criticism, condemnation or judgement denies the reality that God is all souls. Words of love and compassion heal the wounds of others and "others" is our Beloved.

> The first agreement is the most important one and also the most difficult one to honor. It is so important that, with just this first agreement, you will be able to transcend to the level of existence I call heaven on earth. The first agreement is to be impeccable with your word. It sounds very simple, but it is very, very powerful. - Don Miguel Ruiz, *The Four Agreements*

We act in the same way that we speak - ever mindful that our Beloved is in everything. We bring no harm to any person or creature. We act with compassion in the presence of suffering. All of these are ways of loving our Beloved.

> I tell you the truth, whatever you did for one of the least of these brothers of mine, you did for me.
> Jesus – *Matthew* 25:35

Livelihood – our means of providing basic needs should not cause suffering to others. We see our work as work for our Beloved – everything is offered to Him.

Right effort is working to keep our mind on our Beloved at all times.

Mindfulness is to stay ever aware and not fall asleep dreaming about the mansions in our minds. The mind becomes a vessel of love which begins to pour from our hearts to the Beloved like a constant flow of oil. We remain always mindful of this love.

Concentration becomes focused and steady like a candle flame that burns without wavering as though it were in a room with absolutely no air currents.

Perhaps there is no greater influence on our quest for the Divine than other people. This means we should be very careful and discriminating about the company that we choose to keep. In the following commentary by Amma she explains how to keep the right company. It is also poignant with the feeling of intensity that is needed to step beyond the world and into the Heart:

Question: Mother, being a college professor, I have a good circle of friends most of whom are worldly people who talk only about worldly things. How should I deal with them?

Amma: Try to talk less with them, and even then, only if necessary. When they see that you are no longer interested in the things that they are, they will slowly avoid you. Don't think that they will get angry with you; let all of them hate you if they wish. Don't go towards things which will again create trouble for you. You should go towards stillness. Our time is precious. It is not to be wasted by company with others. Whatever time you have, you should be more introspective. Many of the friends come only to gossip and chat, don't they? Lovingly tell them, "We have been talking for a long time. What are we going to gain by talking about and discussing all these things? My goal is to think about God, to give solitude to the mind. You might get angry with me if you don't like it. At present, that is not a problem for me. I can move forward only if I overcome obstacles. I am not angry with you, even if you get angry with me, for I have only love for you. But now I don't have any time to waste." Saying this in a very calm and loving tone, you should withdraw into solitude. Let them love or hate you.

Such control is needed in the beginning. We will become good if we make friends with a river. It will make us reach the ocean. On the other hand, if we keep company with a dirty drain, we will also produce sewage, nothing more than that. Good company is with spiritual people or aspirants and will take us to God. Bad company will make our thoughts and deeds evil. A parrot raised in a temple or church will chant God's Name; whereas a parrot raised in a liquor shop will utter only vulgar words.

If friends come, ask them to stop gossiping and give them spiritual books to read. There is also another way to get out of such situations. Visualize your Beloved Deity in the person who is talking to you. While doing so, you will not even hear what they are saying, although they will feel as if you are listening. In this way you will not be wasting any time. All these restrictions are needed for a seeker of God. We are headed for danger when we see faults in others. Children, bear all this in mind and move carefully.   Amma, *Awaken Children*, vol. 2

Sutra 12 – Steadfast commitment to wisdom

Even after the development of spiritual devotion, there should be steadfast commitment to practicing the wisdom of the scriptures.

bhavatu niscaya-dardhyad urdhvam sastra-raksanam

bhavatu-let there be; *nascaya*-commitment; *dardhyat*-firm resolve; *urdvham*-after; *sastra*-scriptures; *raksanam*-observance

A lover who has merged in the Beloved need not follow any scriptures. There will be no need to follow scriptures as the lover himself has now become the source of all scriptures. Paul echoes this idea:

> The commandments, "Do not commit adultery," "Do not murder," "Do not steal," "Do not covet," and whatever other commandment there may be, are summed up in this one rule: "Love your neighbor as yourself." Love does no harm to its neighbor. Therefore, love is the fulfillment of the law. *Romans 13:9-10, NIV*

However, Narada is not directing this sutra to the perfected siddhas. This is advice for those who have begun to burn and glow with the heat of devotion but have not yet resolved their sense of "I" and "mine." One must continue to follow the scriptural injunctions not only for the practitioner's sake but as an example or encouragement for those around him or her. If one is fortunate enough to have a satguru, then the lover continues to obey the teacher.

I AM A GARDENER

Compassionate Divine Mother
I am a gardener in the flowerbed
    of this universe of beings
These words are my shovel and rake

I am a farmer
    tilling your fields of love
        with the horses of devotion
            and a plow made from poems

What a joy it is to be with you!

What a joy it is to be in love with you!

[From the author's book *Soft Moon Shining*]

Sutra 13 – Danger of a fall

Or else there is danger of taking a fall

anyatha patitya-sankaya

anyatha-otherwise; *patitya*-of falling down; *sankaya*-risk

With spiritual progress there will also come the temptation to fall back into the dream of Maya. In the collective unconscious, all egos of all human beings are united and serve a common cause which is the preservation of the ego. The collective ego will always conspire to pull us from the path whether by an arrangement of external events and circumstances or by the implant of thoughts and emotions that would beckon us to abandon our pursuit. One can avoid this by constant attention to the sacred writings and, if one has a satguru, by strict obedience to the guru's instructions.

Sutra 14 – Body should be preserved

When Divine Love is thoroughly rooted one may give up social forms but the body should be preserved by eating, drinking and wearing protective clothing.

loke pi tavad eva bhojanadi-vyaparas tu a-sarira-dharanavadhi

lokah-in matters of the world; *api*-in addition; *tavat*-for that long; *eva*-indeed; *bhojana*-eating; *adi*-and so on; *vyaparah*-the activity; *tu*-and; *a-sarira-dharana-avadhi*-for as long as the body exists

As long as the devotee is in the world, he should view worldly duties with the same detachment that he holds for the body. Eating, drinking and sleeping are done to provide sustenance for the physical frame and not as a means of entertainment.

Ways of life that are not specifically addressed by the scriptures such as modes of dress and rules of etiquette are of little importance for the siddha (perfected one). Some God realized souls, known as *avadhutas*, may behave very strangely. These holy persons are like fruit trees growing deep in the forest where their fruit is not accessible. Other God realized souls are *bodhisattvas* who incarnate for the purpose of serving humanity and the world. They are generally accessible and will most often observe rules of etiquette in religious and social customs.

Sutra 15 – Differences in point of view

Due to differences in point of view, various descriptions of spiritual devotion have been offered.

tat-laksanani vacyante nana-mata-bhedat

tat-that (bhakti); *laksanani*-the characteristics; *vacyante*-described; *nana*-variously; *mata*-theories; *bhedat*-according to the differences

No words can describe love. It is like a mountain which has a number of paths to attain the peak. Each path on the mountain is different and each has a different landscape to view. A climber on one side of the mountain would give a different account of the view than a climber on the opposite side. Yet the view from the peak is all the same. No particular path can have a complete view.

The following three sutras (16, 17 and 18) indicate paths enjoined to the three levels of creative activity. The three are actions, words and thoughts. Following these is Narada's own description (sutra 19) which is really a revelation of the symptoms of a God-intoxicated person.

Sutra 16 – Ritual worship

Sage Vyasa says a deep and forceful longing to perform ritual worship and ceremonial offerings is the expression of spiritual devotion.

pujadisvanuraga iti Parasaryah

pujadisu-doing ritual worship; *anuragah*-intense longing; *iti*-so thinks; *parasaryah*-Vyasadeva, son of Parasara

Regardless of the simplicity or complexity of the ritual, it is designed to engage all of the worshiper's faculties culminating in single-minded devotion to the Beloved.

> Question: Mother, are rituals like formal worship (puja) necessary? Isn't mental worship enough?
>
> Amma: Son, will hunger be appeased if you merely think of food? Don't you have to eat? In the beginning stages of spiritual life, puja and other ritualistic practices are necessary. They are one way to purify the wandering mind. The wandering nature of the mind can be controlled by keeping it engaged in the remembrance of God or Guru. While cleaning the puja room and puja articles, picking the flowers and making the garland and while doing the puja, the mind will always be thinking of the Lord's worship. This one thought will replace the many disconnected thoughts of the mind and give a sense of quietude. A fixed place, time and materials

for worship are needed at the beginning. Through constant practice, one will reach a stage where one can perform mental worship at all times and places, but this is very subtle and is possible only after the mind has become subtle through concentration and devotion. After this, one will be able to perform every action as a worship of the Lord.   Amma, *Awaken Children*, vol. 1

Sutra 17 – Stories and discussions

According to Sage Garga, delighting in stories of the Beloved and engaging in discussions about the Lord is the hallmark of spiritual devotion.

kathadisu-iti gargah

kathadisu-narrations; *iti*-thus; *gargah*-Sage Gargah Muni

Gargha Muni is a great sage of the bhakti tradition and is said to travel throughout the cosmos expounding on the glories of devotion to the Beloved. He is recommending drinking the nectar of stories of the Lord and participating in conversation about the same. Sri Ramakrishna and Amma would often lapse into a state of Samadhi upon hearing even a few words of a story of the Beloved. Both of these great bhaktas struggled to keep their minds in the physical plane of awareness.

THE GREAT SHAKING

The great shaking begins
With a touch from the Beloved
Where hovers a yearning heart
Floating in the tides of love
Awakened from an ageless sleep
And ends
With the light of eternity
Blazing in the emptiness of space
And filling every thought with love

Sutra 18 – Bliss of the innermost self

And Sage Sandilya recounts that constantly feeling the bliss of the innermost Self is spiritual devotion.

atma-rati-avirodhena-iti-sandilyah

atma-the supreme Self; *rati*-delight; *avirodhena*-ever unobstructed; *iti*-expressed by; *Sandilyah*-Sage Sandilya

It is difficult to comment on the Atman or "innermost Self" in a book dedicated to the subject of bhakti or devotion to God. The Atman or Supreme Self is thought of as being formless – the substratum of all existence.

> Brahmacharin: Mother, what is the nature of Atman?
>
> Mother: No attributes at all. Changeless like the sky. It cannot be said what It is. There is no motion at all. There is no "you" and "I" there. It can be known only if experienced. Amma, *Awaken Children*, vol. 1

Most seekers who follow the path of jnana (contemplation of the formless Self or Atman) abandon the notion of a world, gods, goddesses or anything existing other than the pure formless Self. Upon taking an initial look at this, one might think the practice of bhakti is not applicable. Who is there to worship whom if there is only the one Self?

As an exploration of this sutra we can consider that devotion is not confined to a form and, therefore, we can include love for the formless. As an alternative to this, we can say the formless Atman or Self is never void of form. Therefore, devotion is for the forms that continuously arise out of the formless Atman. We may recall the analogy of paths up a mountain having different views but when the top is reached, it all becomes clear, relevant and unified. When the practitioner reaches the peak, it is found that both of these views are true and not contradictory. Forms that arise out of the formless Atman might include, bliss, light or aliveness.

Practitioners of jnana or non-duality will resist the idea of having devotion for the Atman (Self) because we are the Atman. How can the Self be devoted to itself? Perhaps one answer to this is to understand that all forms are the Self and therefore loving any form of God will lead to the formless Self. Form, when looked at as a whole, that is the sum total of all forms, is eternal.

Adi Shankara (circa 800 CE) is regarded as being the father of modern non-dual philosophy. Most think of him as teaching that there is only the Self or Atman. He also stated in his book *The Crest Jewel of Discrimination* that Maya or form is eternal. He was also a bhakta (lover of God) as well as a jnani (lover of the formless Self). The form of the Divine he worshiped was the Divine Mother. He wrote many hymns and poems of love, devotion and adoration to her.

Ramana Maharshi, a very well-known but deceased jnani or Self realized teacher of non-duality, worshiped the mountain Arunachala where he lived, seeing it as an incarnation of Lord Shiva, and refused to leave it until the day he passed away. Nisargadatta Maharaj, yet another famous but deceased jnani, worshiped a picture of his deceased guru three times a day until Nisargadatta passed away.

These three teachers of jnana (contemplating the formless Self) all worshiped forms as well. That being as it is, we can worship subtler forms such as bliss or light knowing they are intimately connected with the formless Self.

And here is an interesting quote regarding this from Amma:

> Though advaita (the state of non-duality) is the Ultimate Truth, Mother sometimes feels that it is all meaningless and would like to remain like a child in front of God. Amma, *Awaken Children*, vol. 3

This statement sheds light on our dichotomy. The ultimate Truth is pure formless awareness and it is also the universe (form) which is perpetually dancing in the vast open space of awareness. The formless Atman, as pure awareness, is totally still, silent and changeless and it is without beginning or end. Form (the universe), as all that exists, is eternally changing and without beginning or end. Both form and formlessness are eternal. Amma is saying that even though everything is the Self or the Atman, and even though all form is dependent on the Atman, it is still something of a "so what" because there is also no end to form and thus there is no end to love and devotion.

> Brahman (Self) has no name or form. It is infinite like the sky. Knowledge is eternal. When we are in name and form we are in the non-eternal. With his

sankalpa (resolve), the devotee can again do rupa dhyana, that is, meditation on the form of his Beloved Deity even after becoming one with the Absolute." Amma, *Awaken Children*, vol. 2

In conclusion, feeling the bliss of the innermost Self is certainly worthy of our devotion.

Sutra 19 – Deep anguish at forgetting

However, Narada (the author of these sutras) feels that spiritual devotion is the feeling that one is constantly offering every thought, word and deed to the Lord and feeling deep anguish at the least forgetfulness of his Beloved.

Naradastu tadarpitakhilacarata tadvismarane paramavyakulateti

Naradah-Sage Narada; *tu*-however; *tadarpitakhilacarata*-dedication of all actions to the Beloved; *tadvismarane*-on all instances of forgetfulness of the Beloved; *paramavyakulata*-excruciating anguish

The previous three sutras give examples of paths or forms of devotion – ritual worship and ceremonies, telling stories and having discussions about the Beloved and looking inward to the Self. Now Narada is offering his own view. He is also describing the symptoms of devotion. By this sutra we can know if we are making progress.

By dedicating all actions, Narada means we are naturally thinking we are doing every act as an offering of love for the Lord. When we dig in the garden we are giving the work to the Beloved – we are digging and planting for Him or Her. We want the garden to be a gift. If we pour a glass of water, we see the Beloved in the water. Then we offer the water to the Lord and when we drink it we feel the coolness and the taste of the water as if we were a proxy tongue for God – so that God can experience the water with our mouth and tongue. As we drink, we talk to the Lord and ask if He or She is enjoying the water. If we do this with ever action, then we will never experience a moment of not remembering our Beloved. If we do forget, we are immediately pained and the mind and heart are once again pulled back and engaged in the river of love.

As beginners, we are not going to have devotion with this much single-mindedness. However, this is what we should practice and, in time, our single-mindedness will increase. What is wonderful about bhakti, is that we will begin to experience the bliss of the company of the Lord from early on. Amma comments on this:

> There is a benefit in following the path of devotion. One will get bliss from the very beginning itself. Thus one will be encouraged to perform sadhana (spiritual practices)]. In other paths like pranayama (control of the breath), bliss will be gained only at the end. Just as one gets fruit even from the base of a jackfruit tree, bhakti is the path from which one gets fruit from the very beginning onwards. Amma, *Awaken Children*, vol. 2

In the next quote, Amma gives a good description of the intensity that we will reach in the practice of love for our Beloved:

> In the state of pure innocent love, the lover is always hungry. He wants to eat up his beloved. There is an

insatiable hunger in pure love. One can see and experience this intense hunger even in worldly love. But in spiritual love the intensity reaches its peak. That apex is the extreme point, the ultimate limit which is limitless, for this love is all-expansive. In a true seeker this love becomes like a forest fire, yet it is even more intense, more consuming. His whole being will burn with the intensity of that fire of love. In that blazing fire he himself gets consumed and then comes the complete merging.   Amma, *Awaken Children*, vol. 4

And Sri Ramakrishna:

Bankim (to the Master): Sir, how can one develop divine love?

Master: "Through restlessness – the restlessness a child feels for his mother. The child feels bewildered when he is separated from his mother, and weeps longingly for her. If a man can weep like that for God, he can even see Him. Sri Ramakrishna, *The Gospel of Sri Ramakrishna*, p. 674, translated by Swami Nikhilananda

Sutra 20 – Occurrences of sublime devotion

There have been numerous occurrences of this most sublime devotion.

astyevamevam

asti-there is; *evam*-like this; *evam*-like this

The path of bhakti is not common knowledge to those immersed in the illusory pull of the world. It appears in all religions but even then, it is often treated as an unwanted step-child. Bhakti is the first of Jesus' two commandments in which he says to love the Lord your God with all your heart, mind, soul and strength. Unfortunately, an internet search for web sites offering free sermons will reveal that sermons about love for God do not exist.

There are numerous Saints in Christian antiquity that had deep abiding devotion such as St. Francis of Assisi, Padre Pio and Therese Neumann. All three of these had the stigmata in which the wounds of Christ appeared on their hands and feet. Such was the intensity of their love and devotion for Jesus.

Sutra 21 – The Gopis of Vrindavan

The Gopis of Vrindavan had it.

yatha vraja-gopikanam

yatha-as; *vraja*-of Vraja (Vrindavan); *gopikanam*-the cowherd women (Gopis)

In the classic Sanatana Dharma (Hindu) text *Srimad Bhagavatam*, we find a thorough description of the life of Krishna. In his youth, growing up in Vrindavan, there are many stories of his ability to enchant the young women who tended the cows. Even when the Gopis were married, they would all run when they heard Krishna playing his flute. This was a divine attraction as opposed to a boy/girl attraction.

There are many stories to illustrate the perfect devotion that arose out of the Gopi's relationship with Krishna. In one story, Krishna pretended to have a headache and sent Sage Narada to ask Krishna's queens for some dust from their feet. According to Krishna, this was all that could cure his headache. However, it would be very disrespectful to put dirt from one's feet on the Lord and the queens feared retribution from the gods. So they declined to offer any dust. Then Krishna sent Narada to the Gopis with the same request. They did not hesitate and gave the dust to Narada. They were immediately willing to risk whatever ill fate that might result in doing so as long as it brought relief to their Lord. This is an indication of their love for Krishna.

Hanuman's love for Rama is another exemplary relationship between a devotee and the Lord. It is often recounted to show the nature of deep devotion. Rama, like Krishna, was a flesh and bones incarnation of God – an avatar.

Sutra 22 – Do not fall to pride

Even at the highest pinnacle of devotion, one should stay fixed on the glory of the Beloved and not fall to pride which would extinguish the conduit of love.

tatrapi na mahatmyajnanavismrtyapavadah

tatra-there (the highest example of devotion); *api*-even; *na*-not; *mahatmya*-of greatness; *jnana*-of awareness; *vismrti*-of forgetting; *apavadah*-diminishing the relationship

As one progresses with a sense of closeness to the Beloved, one should not forget the greatness of the Beloved and fall into base familiarity. The proper attitude is much like a child to its mother. The child is at once supremely close to its mother yet respects the mother's bigness and her command of every situation. The child never forgets he is not equal to his mother. The wave and the ocean are one but the wave is not the ocean.

We must conclude that pride is the most voracious eater of spiritual aspirants. It is powerful and present on many levels from the gross to the subtle. There are others but they are all too obvious compared to pride – anger, greed, attachment, jealousy.

Everyone has pride whereas some may not have greed or anger. If someone insults us or reprimands us and we feel hurt - that is pride. Pride is self-importance and is found at the root of one's own perception of being either inferior or superior. If a person suffers from "miserable wretched sinner" syndrome it is because of self-cherishing which is an undue obsession with one's own ego. The flow is like this, "I am important and so it is just awful that I am such a sinner and this makes me a bad person."

If self-importance were absent, one would not be concerned with being either a sinner or a saint. It should be noted that one who has diminished self-importance will also behave in the world in a selfless way expressing love and compassion naturally. Self-importance is contrary to love and compassion because self-importance is all about "me" leaving no room to care for the happiness of others.

For the seeker, the person on the path, it is guaranteed that the first glimmer of success will invite the ego to assert itself. Pride appears and we are off and running to the end zone of perdition.

The ego needs to be different in order to define itself and religion and politics are perfect for this. We, the practitioner, have experiences or gain book knowledge and it is all too easy to contrast this with the oceans of people in the world that we feel are "clueless." We now know something they don't know and this makes us special.

If we have the company of a satguru, we need not be too concerned with this as the guru will make corrections. Editing oneself is most difficult and requires utmost attention including studying scriptures and reading the words of saints. We all know how easy it is to see the faults of others but for our own frailties were are as blind as bats. If someone is rude to us, we should welcome the experience as an opportunity to see how much progress we are making. If we have no reaction, we are doing well.

Some ways that pride comes to bear are being argumentative, clinging to one's opinions, wanting to control others, being a know-it-all, being inflexible, impatience, pickiness, excessive talking, my way or the highway, inability to hear what others are saying, feeling like an expert and being judgmental toward others. Pride prevents us from making progress on our path. We set out as beginners in our little canoe and as soon as we have gone a small distance pride comes like a huge rock falling out of the sky and makes a big hole in our canoe causing us to sink. And we are not even aware that it has happened!

God's grace will flow only when there is humility. Why is this? God is everything including all other people. Spiritual progress is measured as the amount of illusory separation we have removed from our minds. Pride causes the opposite – it increases the feeling of separation. Not only separate from others and from Nature but from our Beloved. The very nature of pride is separateness. If I am special or important, then I am separate. I can only be special if there is something other than me that provides contrast. I am this and that is that. I am spiritual and they are asleep. I am of a better religion and their religion is not so good. I know things and they do not.

Pride, then, is a wall we build around ourselves. Another unfortunate aspect of pride is that it is so intoxicating to the ego. Like heroin, it smooths over all the inconvenient bumps on the road to self-cherishing which becomes self-worshiping. Unfortunately, we end up being separated from everyone and everything including God. We will find ourselves alone, destitute and pounded by the storms of life.

Amma comments on the dangers that lie in the rapids:

> When you think that you have attained Realization, the very worst will start happening. Slowly and furtively the ego will enter. You won't see him coming in. You won't recognize him, and even if you do recognize him, you won't care because you will be so enamored of the idea that you are truly realized. Thus you will try to overlook his trickery. Or you may feel, 'This is how it is after Realization.' So you start enjoying old habits and indulging in old pleasures, and so you fall back into the world.
>
> Children, you don't have any idea about how life will be after Realization because you are not realized. As far as you are concerned, the state is totally unknown. You are simply assuming that you are realized, but there is no ground for this assumption. A sadhak (spiritual aspirant) who makes this assumption, who feels he is already realized, is wrong. There are no feelings in that state. Even the thought 'I have reached' will not exist.

However, if you feel this, then that is another thought which will block your path. You have not yet attained the state of Perfection, for Truth is far beyond. But to convince you of this, to show you the Truth, a Satguru is needed. The Guru's grace is absolutely necessary. Amma, *Awaken Children*, vol. 5

Nisargadatta Maharaj also corroborates this theme:

There are so many who take the dawn for the noon, a momentary experience for full realisation and destroy even the little they gain by excess of pride. Humility and silence are essential for a sadhaka, however advanced. Only a fully ripened jnani can allow himself complete spontaneity. – Nisargadatta Maharaj, *I Am That*

And another comment by Amma on pride:

Real greatness lies in humility and simplicity. The friendship of God, the Servant, can be gained only if the ego and false pride are removed. At present we sit with the pride of a chieftain. Our attitude should become like that of a servant. We should become more humble than anything else. We should remove the ego and then He will come running to us. There is no other way to attain God. - Amma, *Awaken Children*, vol. 2

Love is the most potent destroyer of ego and pride. This is an advantage the path of bhakti (spiritual devotion) has over the path of jnana (knowledge of the Self). The devotee is always in the presence of something greater than himself which is the Beloved.

It is very difficult for someone to wake up who is dreaming they are awake.

"You must ask God to give you power to fight against the sin of pride which is your greatest enemy – the root of all that is evil, and the failure of all that is good. For God resists the proud." - St. Vincent de Paul

Sutra 23 – Love which fails to bow

Love which fails to bow to the glory of the Beloved is no more than the self-cherishing love of an unchaste person for his or her paramour.

tadvihinam jaranamiva

tadvihinam-lack of awareness of the Beloved's greatness; *jaranam*-illicit lovers; *iva*-as

This sutra continues the theme of the one prior to it. A devotee must continue to bow to the greatness of the Lord. At the point of merging with the Beloved, the lover ceases to be a separate person and so this is the pinnacle of humility. The path then is ever increasing humility which is cultivated by ceaselessly contemplating the greatness and the glory of our Beloved.

Here Narada compares devotion without awe as a wholly selfish act such as a sexual predator might have for his/her next conquest. Pure spiritual love does not expect or want anything in return. One loves the various aspects of the Beloved such as beauty, wisdom, compassion, mystery, omnipotence and so on. Overwhelmed by such greatness one bows with a heart brimming with love. If this awestruck auspiciousness is absent, devotion degenerates into selfish bargaining. The devotee begins to consider what can be gained and how to get it.

Sutra 24 – About selfish love

In selfish love, there is no concern for the happiness of the paramour.

nastyeva tasmin tatsukhasukhitvam

na-not; asti-there is; *eva*-indeed; *tasmin*-in it; *tat*-that, the Beloved; *sukha*-in the happiness; *sukhitvam*-personal happiness

When the mind is focused on satisfying desires then there can really be no love. If we say we love ice cream, it is not really love but desire and the need to satisfy the desire. If one is immersed in the illusion that pleasure is the same as happiness then the sense of separation will be our lot. From this will follow an unending reign of misery and suffering.

The path of devotion is to remove this illusion and to diminish the sense of self-cherishing. This is accomplished by cultivating pure love for the Beloved. At first our efforts will be mixed with impurities. The very thought of pursuing bhakti to destroy our illusions is self-centered. However, by persevering in this direction, the mind and heart will gradually become pure and love will be of the selfless kind.

> Suppose there is some red-colored water in a vessel. If you go on adding fresh water to it, the red color will slowly become less until at last it completely disappears. Likewise, all bad thoughts can be gotten

rid of by cultivating and developing good thoughts.
Amma, *Awaken Children*, vol. 1

Sri Ramakrishna comments:

Brahmo devotee: What is the sign of one who has attained true wisdom living in the world?

Ramakrishna: When the repetition of the Name of the Lord will bring tears to the eyes, send a thrill through the whole body and make the hair stand on end. The spiritual eye must be opened. It is open when the mind is purified. Then the presence of Divinity will be realized everywhere and every woman will appear as Divine Mother. Everything is in the mind. The impure mind brings attachment to the world, and the purified mind brings the realization of God. The impure mind of a man becomes attached to a woman. Woman naturally loves man and man naturally loves woman, and from this spring attachment and worldliness. *Gospel of Ramakrishna*, translated by Swami Abhedananda.

Sutra 25 – Bhakti the greatest path

Devotion for the Beloved (bhakti yoga) is greater than the yogas of service (karma yoga), knowledge (jnana yoga) and traditional raja yoga.

sa tu karmajnanayogebhyo 'py adhikatara

sa- that (bhakti); *tu-*but; karma-action as service; *jnana-*knowledge, gnosis; *yogebhyah-*mystic meditation; *api-*indeed; *adhikatara-*superior to

To follow are three words from the Bible that explain why Narada says bhakti is the most exalted of all the paths.

God is love.   1 John 4:8

There are no intellectual handles for love. It is utterly formless and subjective. For this reason, persons who primarily dwell in their intellect will dismiss love. It is not so much that they purposefully dismiss it as they just don't see it. One has to put on love glasses in order to see the love in everything. Conversely, the intellect can find much cud to chew on the other paths. In one sense, it is as if the other paths are necessarily there to entertain the mind with engaging concepts, labyrinths of details, fascinating planes of existence and titillating energy rushes in the same way a child is given toys. This is useful for those who are beholden to their intellects as it keeps them spiritually occupied until such a time as they are able to embrace love. The intellect must be left behind to know love. These diversions continue until the heart begins to shine with

89

pure selfless love. At that point every path becomes a path of love. Every path becomes bhakti and all complexities fade away. This is why Narada says bhakti is the most noble path.

This is not to speak dismissively about these paths as they are all wonderful. However, we can consider that they are unnecessarily indirect and circuitous when compared to the path of love. A person who is not acquainted with Divine Love will have a hard time agreeing with this. It would be like saying to a person who has never tasted chocolate, "Chocolate tastes better than gruel." How would they ever know? Being attached to their consumption of gruel, they will defend it.

Love is the basis of existence itself therefore love is the ultimate fulfillment. Love is the first step, the middle step and the last step. There is no way to describe the bliss of pure selfless love. Once it is tasted, one knows there is nothing else. The state of Love is profound stillness yet it is radiant and self-luminous like pure evenly flowing light. Even the flowing seems still because it is so constant like a waterfall seems still even though it is moving. Stillness is alive, emptiness is creative, the universe is bliss, and awareness is love.

Amma comments:

> Another man: Is Raja Yoga the best path?
>
> Amma: Children, it is difficult to say "such and such" a path is good and "such and such" is not a

good one. All paths are equally good if they are properly practiced with the right understanding. Anyhow, just one path cannot be advised for all people since people are different mentally, physically, and intellectually. The spiritual disposition inherited by the aspirant from the previous birth is the criteria to test which path is good for a person. Though all paths are equally good, each one works differently in different people. Each person will have a spontaneous feeling or inclination towards a particular path and that will be the correct path for him. In any case, to be on the safe side, it is better to approach a Satguru in order to find one's path, to determine which direction one should go, to discover who is our Beloved Deity and to obtain other advice for one's spiritual growth.

Children, as far as Mother is concerned, the path of devotion is the best and the easiest since most people are predominately emotional in nature. Not only that, bhakti marga (path of devotion) has no complications like the other paths. There are no harmful techniques or complications involved in love. Simply love the Lord. Love is not aggressive; it is a constant flow.

It is always dangerous to do sadhana after reading books. Always be aware that those who write books and give speeches are not all Gurus. Try to follow the footsteps of those who have fully experienced what they say or write about.

Question: Kundalini will rise through the practice of Hatha Yoga, won't it?

Amma: Why do you think about all these complicated methods when there are easier ones? Hatha Yoga should be practiced under the strict guidance of a Perfect Master. You cannot simply adopt any method that you feel like. Each one will have a path which they would have followed in the previous birth. Only if that path is followed will one progress in one's practice.

If Hatha Yoga is practiced by oneself, it might lead to the danger of becoming more aware of the body and thus will inflate the ego. Whereas, the sole aim of spiritual practice is to get rid of this body-consciousness. Whichever is the path, it is enough to gain concentration. The concept about kundalini rising is a bhavana (creative imagination). We can have the concept about God as well. It is the same idea. Whether you follow the path of devotion or the path of karma or the path of jnana, this awakening of the kundalini must happen. The difference is that a devotee calls the same kundalini shakti as Krishna, Rama, Devi, Jesus or Buddha. Children, do your sadhana properly and sincerely. Do not waste your energy and time thinking, "When is the kundalini going to awaken? Will it rise up if I follow this path or is the other path better?"   Amma, *Awaken Children*, vol. 3

Like raja yoga, the path of jnana yoga is chained to the concept of doing this practice for "me." The practice is all for one's self and all about one's self. There is a goal in mind. It is most difficult to untangle the self from the Self. For example, one desires to be free from the delusional ego. This desire is necessary at first in the practice of jnana yoga. It is impossible for most to have any success with this unless they are under the tutelage of a satguru or perfect master. The jnani must wait until self-realization to know any bliss.

A self-realized jnani who has reached the state of perfect spontaneity will understand love. Nisargadatta Maharaj, a well-known but deceased jnana yogi, often talks about love in the book *I Am That*. His comments about love are usually overlooked by the dry intellects who study and comment on his words. Nisargadatta comments:

> Questioner: You seem to be so very indifferent to everything!
>
> Maharaj: I am not indifferent, I am impartial. I give no preference to the me and the mine. A basket of earth and a basket of jewels are both unwanted. Life and death are all the same to me.
>
> Questioner: Impartiality makes you indifferent.
>
> Maharaj: On the contrary, compassion and love are my very core. Void of all predilections, I am free to love.

Sri Ramakrishna said:

> To know God through jnana and reasoning is
> extremely difficult. Ramakrishna, *The Gospel of
> Ramakrishna*, p. 94

Karma yoga is less prone to self-centered desires because
actions are dedicated to the Lord and are often motivated
by compassion. Karma yoga can more easily be seen as a
stepping stone to bhakti.

Amma comments again:

> But generally speaking, the Path of Devotion is the
> easiest and the least complicated. While anybody
> can love, not all can do pranayama (breath control)
> or Hatha Yoga (yogic postures). Only certain people
> endowed with a certain mental and physical
> constitution can do these. But love has no
> prerequisites. Whoever has a heart can love, and
> everyone has a heart. To love is an innate tendency
> in human beings. However, we cannot say that
> pranayama or Hatha Yoga come naturally to human
> beings. Bhakti is love – loving God, loving your own
> Self, and loving all beings. The small heart should
> become bigger and bigger and, eventually, totally
> expansive. A spark can become a forest fire. So to
> have only a spark is enough, for the spark is also
> fire. Keep blowing on it, fanning it. Sooner or later it
> will burn like a forest fire, sending out long tongues
> of flame. At present, love is like a spark within us.
> Constantly blow on it, using the fan of the Divine

Name, japa and meditation. You may perspire, sneeze and cough, but do not stop. Your body may become hot; tears may fill your eyes; you may want to faint. But do not stop. If you perspire, you sneeze and cough, persist in your efforts, and be assured then that you are heading towards the goal. Soon you will become Love itself. This is the reward for your love.   Amma, *Awaken Children*, vol. 4

Ramakrishna comments that *Prema* or ecstatic love is absolutely the highest state of spirituality:

The first stage of spiritual practice is association with spiritual people, the company of holy men. The second stage is faith in things relating to the Spirit. The third stage is single-minded devotion to one's Ideal. The Ideal may be one's Guru, the spiritual teacher, the Impersonal Brahman, the Personal God or any of His manifestations. The fourth stage is the state of being struck speechless at the thought of God. The fifth stage, when the feeling of devotion to God reaches the highest point; it is called *Mahabhava*. The devotee sometimes laughs, sometimes weeps like a madman. He loses all control over his body. This state is not attained by ordinary human beings who are not capable of conquering the flesh. It is reached by Incarnations of God who appear in this world for the salvation of mankind. The sixth stage, Prema or ecstatic love, goes hand in hand with Mahabhava. It is the most intense love of God and is strictly the highest state of spirituality. The two marks of this stage are the forgetfulness of this world and the forgetfulness of self, which includes one's own body. *Gospel of Ramakrishna,* translated by Swami Abhedananda

From Sri Krishna

And I consider the yogi-devotee who lovingly contemplates on Me with supreme faith, and whose mind is ever absorbed in Me to be the best of all the yogis. *Bhagavad Gita* 6.47

Sutra 26 – Bliss from the beginning

Devotion is greater because the bliss of devotion is itself the fruit and is available from the beginning of the path. Pure, selfless love and devotion are the eventual goal of all other paths.

phalarupatvat

phala-fruit; *rupatvat*-because it is the nature or form of the end result

The bhakta gets immediate feedback and satisfaction in the bliss that is felt. This provides continuous encouragement for the practice. The devotee will immediately be invited into the living room of God's heart. The lover of God is given a permanent backstage pass. All others practicing other paths must wait outside until the point of realization.

Because pure, selfless love and devotion are the goal of every spiritual path, one can derive the most benefit from the path of bhakti or spiritual devotion. Bhakti is the most direct path. The goal is experienced even at the very beginning. There only remains the process of cultivating love and devotion from a small flame to a roaring bonfire. The fire in the flame and the bonfire are the same and differ only in intensity.

FLYING FLAGS OF LOVE

Mother of light
Our very beings
Have breached the dam
Of these threadbare bags
Of flesh and bone
Joyously spilling
Into the stark emptiness
And utter aliveness
That sparkles in your finger tips

Your children
Wander spellbound
Drunk and singing
Old pilgrim songs of bliss
Drinking the starlight
From your ever exploding
Om filled heart

There is no universe
That can hold
Your astonishing
Flying flags of love
Filling space and time
With the rapture
Of your mind destroying
Hammers of silence

[From the author's book *Divine Mother of the Universe*]

98

Sutra 27 – Lord cherishes humility

Love for the Beloved is also highest because the Lord cherishes humility and runs away from egotism.

isvarasyapi-abhimana-dvesitvat dainya-priyatvacca

isvarasya-of the Supreme Lord; *api*-also; *abhimani*-of those who are proud; *dvesitvat*-one who dislikes; *dainya*-of humility; *priyatvacca*-because of being drawn to

The very nature of egotism is separateness. This creates two major obstacles. The first is that our sense of separateness will exclude God from our world. For the egotist, not only God but Nature and everyone they know are excluded. Because we mistakenly identify with our bodies we construct a world in our minds in which we are separate. In this way, we ourselves block the grace of the Beloved that is continuously flowing at all times. Our separateness does not allow us to be receptive.

The second factor to consider is that God's very nature is love and compassion. If we have the attitude of a beginner who has realized one's helplessness and if we call to God with a sincere heart, God's compassion will not be able to resist.

The danger of pride and egotism is always more prevalent in the other paths. A small amount of success and our ego is ready to claim it. This is, unfortunately, the nature of the ego and we all have one. Bhakti is the only path that does not have personal benefit as a goal.

99

One who thinks of the Lord with an unwavering mind and a heart overflowing with love and devotion for God, is undoubtedly taken care of by the Lord.

> God will not reside where there is ego and selfishness. If these are there, God will move a thousand feet away from us. He will come close if we call sincerely. Amma, *Awaken Children*, vol. 2

And the best way to learn humility:

> When death comes, we are helpless. The constant remembrance of the possibility of death is the best way to learn humility. Amma, *Awaken Children*, vol. 6

Sutra 28 – Some say the path of knowledge

Some say spiritual devotion is attainable through the path of knowledge of the Beloved.

tasyah jnanam eva sadhanamityeke

tasyah-about bhakti; *jnanam*-knowledge; *eva*-solely; *sadhanam*-the means; *iti*-thus; *eke*-some

There is some cursory justification for pursuing the path of knowledge or jnana as a stepping stone to devotion. It is reasoned that one cannot just fall in love with something unknown and so Self inquiry will provide that introduction. However, the Self that is the target for those on the path of jnana, is pure, formless awareness and it is not something one can love. In fact, it is our own Self!

Yes, it is true that everything is the Self, however it is also true that everything as form or as a personal God, is also eternally existing. This is stated by Adi Shankara, the father of modern jnana philosophy, in his *Crest Jewel of Discrimination*. To know the personal aspect of the eternal, the path of jnana or knowledge will not take us there. Knowing the eternal as a person is a higher revelation than jnana knowing the Self. This is experiencing the entire universe as a living, conscious, willful and intelligent being who is capable of communicating with us and loving us.

The following quote by Amma was posted earlier in Sutra 18 but it is worth reading again because it is so revealing of this deep mystery:

Though advaita (the state of non-duality or jnana) is the Ultimate Truth, Mother sometimes feels that it is all meaningless and would like to remain like a child in front of God.   Amma, *Awaken Children*, vol. 3

What is needed to introduce one to the Lord is love and not knowledge. God *is* love. This is why one can succeed by picking any image of God and making an attempt to feel love for God in that form. We do this with a process that is akin to visualizing but we do it with our feelings. This is explained in detail in the author's book *Finding God's Love*. God will then appear to the devotee first as a feeling of returning love and then in a more palpable sense.

Some book knowledge is useful to begin the practice of bhakti and this book is evidence of that. Also, details about one's chosen form are useful to some extent. However, none of these empirical details will be sufficient to step into the river of love. They can only tell us how to find the river.

THE LOVE OF GOD

Could we with ink the ocean fill,
Were every blade of grass a quill,
Were the world of parchment made,
And every man a scribe by trade,
To write the love of God above
Would drain the ocean dry;
Nor would the scroll contain the whole,
Though stretched from sky to sky.

- by Unkown Author

Sutra 29 – Some say devotion and knowledge

Some say devotion and knowledge are both necessary.

anyonyasrayatvam ity eke

anyonya-mutual; *asrayatvam*-dependance; *iti*-thus (declare); *eke*-some

Devotion is necessary for the path of jnana or knowledge. In order to practice this path, one must be devoted to the one primal Self of existence – which is everyone's own Self. This devotion must be there to find the motivation to proceed with a very dry path. One must walk across a vast desert wasteland in order to eventually find the oasis that contains the blissful wellspring of existence we call the Self (I AM THAT I AM in the Bible).

Non-dual knowledge of the Self is not necessary to proceed with bhakti - the path of spiritual devotion. Love for the Beloved is sufficient as long as one understands the Beloved is in all things, everyone and that the entire universe is the body of God. Without this understanding, one's view could devolve into fanaticism born of segmented thinking that leads us to the mistaken belief that our view is the only view. One could say this understanding of the omnipresence of the Beloved is a necessary spice in the stew of bhakti.

While we can assert that God realization or Self-realization will result in the simultaneous understanding of knowledge (gnosis) and spiritual devotion, Narada is saying that the path to that peak by way of devotion does not require the practice of jnana.

A true master who is the product of the path of knowledge of the Self will also embrace devotion in the end. However, few practitioners of this path will ever arrive at this pinnacle. Here are a few who did: Ramana Maharshi wrote a treatise on the practice of devotion. He regarded the mountain Arunachala as an incarnation of Lord Shiva and worshiped it until the day he died. Nisargadatta Maharaj worshiped a picture of his guru three times a day (his guru had long since passed away) until the point that Nisargadatta left his body. Shankaracharya (circa 800 C.E.) is regarded as the father of modern non-dual (jnana) philosophy. Yet he fervently worshiped God in the form of the Divine Mother and wrote many hymns and poems of devotion and adoration to her. However, these mahatmas were the exception. By and large, a great percentage of persons attempting the path of jnana will never succeed. The premise is simple but the practice is most difficult. The pitfalls and problems with this path are discussed in greater detail in an appendix at the end of this book. Amma comments:

> Once Narada saw a strong effulgence. He went near it and found that it was Jnana Devata performing penance. He asked upon whom She was meditating. She replied that She was meditating on the Lotus Feet of the Lord. Here also, the importance is stressed for bhakti. Jnana will not be received by a person who has no devotion. In that sense, one can

say that both bhakti and jnana are one and the same. Amma, *Awaken Children*, vol. 3

More quotes from Amma regarding this:

Bhakti is not different from jnana. Real devotion is itself wisdom.   Amma, *Awaken Children*, vol. 1

Bhakti and jnana, though seemingly different, are not two. Bhakti is the means and jnana the end. Bhakti without jnana and jnana without bhakti are both harmful. In fact, bhakti is the easiest and least complicated way. Anyone and everyone can follow it. Bhakti culminates in jnana. The Lord of a true devotee and Brahman, the Absolute Reality of the Jnani, are really one and the same.   Amma, Awaken Children, vol. 1

Sutra 30 – Love is its own reward

Narada, the son of Brahma, says love for the Beloved is its own reward.

svayam phalarupateti Brahmakumarah

svayam-of itself; *phalarupateti*-becoming its own fruit; *iti*-thus; *Brahmakumarah*-son of Brahma (Narada)

> The state that we attain by calling and crying to God is equal to the bliss that the yogi experiences in samadhi. Amma, *Awaken Children*, vol. 3

Swami Amritaswarupananda comments on Amma's continuous state of Divine Grace:

> As described by the great sage Narada, all the signs of parabhakti (supreme devotion) are manifest in the Holy Mother. For instance, in the days when She was performing sadhana (spiritual practice) to realize the Divine Mother, She would suffer excruciating pain of separation from God. If She happened to forget the Divine Name even for a single moment She would feel extremely dejected thinking of the lost time. To make up for that, She would chant or meditate with more intensity. Mother would also see everything as Devi (Divine Mother) and in that mood She would embrace the trees actually feeling them to be Devi. Sometimes She would sit for a long time on the banks of the

107

backwaters touching Her nose on the surface of the water as if kissing the ripples. If She happened to see any women or girls dressed in sarees at this time, Mother would run to them and embrace them calling "Amma...Amma!". Now the Holy Mother was sharing Her own experiences with Her children and devotees. She said, "Even now I am struggling hard to keep my mind down, especially while singing bhajans. It is always shooting up." Swami Amritaswarupananda, *Awaken Children*, vol. 1

Sutra 31 – Observe examples of king, home

We can observe this in the examples of a king, a home, food and so on.

rajagrahbhojanadisu tathaiva drstatvat

rajan-king; *grahm*-residence; *bhojanadisu*-in a meal and so on; *tathaiva*-in just this way; *drstatvat*-it is seen

Sutras 31 and 32 are really the same thought.

Narada continues to make the case that knowledge will not lead to devotion. However, this knowledge may be different than the jnana knowledge in the previous sutras. The knowledge referred to here may be empirical knowledge as opposed to jnana or experiential knowing (gnosis). The word *jnana* is not in this sutra or the next. Also, empirical knowledge would fit with the point in the next sutra. Empirical knowledge would be factoids and observations. We can observe what electricity does as it affects the world but to experience it directly we have to grab hold of a live wire.

Sutra 32 – Knowledge does not provide

Knowledge does not make one royalty, satisfy one or remove hunger.

na tena raja paritosah ksucchantirva

na-not; *tena*-by that (knowledge); *raja*-of the king; *paritosah*-satisfaction; *ksucchantih*-removal of hunger; *va*-or

Sutras are by definition short. We could add a few words to this one for clarification:

Knowing facts about the Lord does not make one a devotee in the same way that living in a palace does not make one a king, standing in a blueprint does not give one a home and having a cook book does not remove hunger. Amma is also found of saying one cannot write honey on a piece of paper and then lick it expecting to taste sweetness. Only the experience of love for the Beloved makes one a devotee. This is a baptism with tears of profound joy.

Sutra 33 – Path of devotion alone is suitable

Therefore, the path of devotion alone is suitable for those who long to be free.

tasmat saiva grahya mumuksubhih

tasmat-therefore; *sa*-it (bhakti); *eva*-only; *grahya*-worthy of attaining; *mumuksubhih*-those who work towards liberation

This sutra marks the end of Narada's comparison of knowledge and devotion.

Love for the Divine is the goal of human existence. Practitioners of jnana (knowledge of the Self) will take issue with this. They are taught that there is only the pure, formless Self and that the universe and all forms anywhere are an illusion. They have the idea that eternity is wholly impersonal but this is only because they have yet to meet Her.

Bhakti and jnana are both paths to the Truth. Because jnana is such a difficult practice and because, as Amma states, only a few will ever realize the goal with this path, we can say that bhakti is the only suitable path for those that long to be liberated from Samsara (the seemingly endless cycles of birth and death).

Jnana is like a single rare tree that grows only on a desert island off the coast of Madagascar and bears only one or two fruits once every 20 years. By comparison, bhakti is a lush orchard of fruit trees stretching as far as the eye can see. Each bears bushels of fruit twice a year without fail. One can go either way and it is true that liberation is available in either direction.

The path of jnana proposes a simple concept: We are limitless, formless, pure awareness. However, experiencing this permanently is most difficult. For those wishing to look more closely, we have included, at the end of this book, a chapter on the problems in practicing the path of Self-knowledge (a.k.a. jnana, advaita, non-duality). It was originally printed in the author's book *Into The Mystic*.

WHY DISAPPEAR INTO FORMLESS TRANCE?

O wavering mind
awaken your upward flowing awareness.
Become the sublime warrior Goddess Kali,
who moves with graceful power
   through the vast landscape of the body.

Her divine form, like a black storm cloud
   illumined by the sun,
she stands unveiled,
her long hair falling free like monsoon rain.
Be lost in awe of her, O mind,
for you will never comprehend her.

She dwells as the primal lotus of conscious energy
   and also as the thousand petal blossom,

complete enlightenment.
She is none other than primordial bliss,
This great swan ever swimming
    through the lotus jungle of the subtle body.

Gaze intently into the blazing heart of joy
    and you will perceive my blissful Mother,
matrix of all phenomena.

The vision of Kali
    kindles the fire of unitive wisdom,
burning down conventional barriers,
pervading minds and worlds with light,
revealing her exalted beauty
    as a universal flower garden
and universal cremation ground,
where lovers merge with Mother Reality,
experiencing the single taste of non-duality.

This ardent poet of the Goddess cries:
"Every lover longs only to gaze upon the unique Beloved.
Why close your eyes?
Why disappear into formless trance?"

[From *Mother of the Universe*, poetry of Ramprasad
translated by Lex Hixon, Quest Books]

Sutra 34 – Great teachers of devotion

Great teachers have shown the path of devotion for the Beloved.

tasyah sadhanani gayantyacaryah

tasyah-about this (bhakti); *sadhanani*-means of cultivating; *gayanti*-sing; *acaryah*-the great teachers

Prior to this sutra Narada has been mostly talking about the "why" of bhakti. He is telling us why it is better and why we would want to pursue it. From here on, Narada will be discussing how to develop love for our Beloved.

It should be noted that Narada uses the word *sing* in this sutra. This is to express the innocent joy that flows from these great teachers of bhakti. They are singing like birds in the forest and are motivated by nothing more than love.

Bhakti is a means to purify the mind and the emotions. An emotion is an intense and concentrated thought. Cessation of all thought is the end result as one swims in the ocean of bliss illumined as it were with a cool, peaceful radiance that is also intensely alive. It is beyond imagining. A feeling of perpetual joy literally flows through the nervous system. A satguru or perfect master will always be happy. For them, the entire universe is no more than a feather on the back of an elephant.

> Life should become one big, hearty laugh - that is religion. That's spirituality. That is real prayer. God is the innocent smile that blossoms from within.   - Amma

As we walk along the path of devotion we can watch for symptoms of our progress. We stop taking the world seriously; we stop taking ourselves so seriously; we are happy and joyous; we are fearless as we have taken refuge in our Beloved; every day we are taking truckloads of our attachments to the dump; we feel light and free in our new found humility!

Mental and emotional impurities are anything that agitate the mind or distract the mind from the Beloved. These weeds must be pulled out for devotion to root. Love and devotion will naturally subdue these impurities but getting the love going in the beginning will require effort to reduce the impurities enough that we can fan the spark into a flame.

These impurities are like water that has soaked into our firewood. It is very difficult to get the wood to burn initially. Once the wood begins to burn, the flame will, itself, begin to dry the remaining wood thus removing the remaining impurities. The dryer the surrounding wood becomes, the hotter and faster the fire burns. The initial beginning period requires some intensity and focus on the part of the practitioner. It is like leaving the earth in a rocket. At first a tremendous amount of energy must be expended to get the rocket beyond the pull of the earth's gravity. Once in space, movement is effortless and occurs with no resistance.

Devotion is a means and it is the end. It leads to Parabhakti or Supreme Love. This is God-realization itself.

GREAT TEACHERS OF BHAKTI

Like dark swollen rain clouds
These great teachers
Gather their lightning bolts
Few can see them
But those that do
Will never be the same

Sutra 35 – Attachment to objects of the senses

To develop love for the Beloved, it is vital to abandon fascination for and attachment to the myriad of objects that come and go in the five senses.

tat tu visaya-tyagat sangatyagat ca

tat-that (bhakti); *tu*-and; *visaya*-objects of the senses; *tyagat*-by renouncing; *sanga*-of physical association or dependence; *tyagat*-by renouncing; *ca*-and

> Whoever it may be, without renunciation one cannot realize God. Amma, *Awaken Children*, vol. 1

If cultivating love for the Lord is the quintessential "do" then attachment to the objects of the senses a.k.a. the world – El Mundo – is the quintessential "don't."

Desire and aversion are both forms of attachment. Desire for one object also creates aversions to other objects that might prevent us from possessing the object we desire. For example, we want an ice cream cone and we need it now! We are 12 years old and the nearest ice cream is 10 miles away. Our mom is the only one home and she has a car and would probably take us. Suddenly our grandmother calls and we know it's going to be a long conversation and our mom has to go to work in an hour. In this case our attachment to ice cream is being thwarted and so we have an aversion to the fact that our grandmother has just called our mom. We think, "Oh, nooooo!" This play of desires and aversions creates a very fragmented view of the world

117

which seems to be full of disconnected objects and events. We want "this" but don't want "that." This view is contrary to reality in which everything in the universe is the Beloved. As lovers of God, we will be attempting to see everything that life gives us as being given to us by the Beloved. We are going to practice non-attachment to do this.

Non-attachment is not indifference.

Merriam-Webster's dictionary defines indifference: "Lack of interest in or concern about something : an indifferent attitude or feeling."

Indifference is the disease of not being able to see the difference between a rock and a human. One may ask if this is not what spirituality teaches? That God is in everything and everything is God which means there is no difference between a rock and a human?

A person who sees God in everything will love and respect everything and will express compassion to those that suffer. Indifference is the opposite. Indifference is the inability to see anything as being sacred or lovable other than one's self or ego. Thus, anything other than one's self is nothing more than a box of rocks to be treated in whatever way suits our mood at the time.

Indifference is the result of an ego-centered, self-cherishing outlook. Indifference is the absence of love and compassion. If another person is suffering, we feel no compassion. If an animal is suffering, we feel no compassion. There is no sense of caring for others and wishing them to be happy. This ego-centered view breeds anger, hatred, greed, jealousy, pride and so on. If we look closely, we can see that these negative traits are all about 'me." Indifference leads us to think we must get ours first before someone else gets it. It is a view of utter separation. Other people are seen as nothing more than objects to satisfy our desires.

A sociopath is the end result of indifference. Such a person has no conscience and certainly no love or compassion.

Indifference is not the same as detachment or non-attachment discussed in spiritual texts. They are actually opposites. Non-attachment is the removal of the ego with its likes and dislikes. The result of this is to be able to say "Yes" to all of life; to embrace life with unconditional love. In fact, unconditional love is not possible without non-attachment. Indifference is the triumph of the ego while non-attachment is the triumph of love.

Another reason that we want to renounce our attachment to the objects of the senses is that these are distracting and constantly keep our attention in an outward flowing extroverted mode. We will have little or no time for our Beloved who dwells on the throne of our heart. To experience our Beloved directly, to feel the waves of love and bliss, we must be looking inward. Our fascination with the things of the world will also dissipate the reserves of spiritual energy that we might have accumulated.

Amma likes to use an analogy of sugar and ants to illustrated this. We do spiritual practices, feel love for our Beloved and this produces "sugar." Then we indulge in pleasures and habitual interests which are the ants that eat our sugar.

> Colors blind the eye
> Sounds deafen the ear
> Flavors numb the taste
> Thoughts weaken the mind
> Desires whither the heart
>
> The Master observes the world
> But trusts his inner vision
> He allows things to come and go
> His heart is as open as the sky
>
> *Tao Te Ching* translated by Stephen Mitchell

Allowing things to come and go is the essence of non-attachment. Paramahamsa Ramakrishna comments:

> Then turning towards Visvanatha and His numerous devotees, Ramakrishna said: Meditate upon God, the sole Existence, Knowledge and Bliss Eternal, and you also shall have bliss. That Being of Knowledge and Bliss is always here and everywhere, only It is covered and obscured by ignorance. The less is your attachment towards the senses, the more will be your love for God. *Gospel of Ramakrishna,* translated by Swami Abhedananda

Sri Krishna tells Arjuna (Kaunteya) about control (non-attachment) of the senses:

> For the senses are so turbulent, O Kaunteya, that they forcibly seize the mind of even a wise individual who perseveres. The disciplined individual should restrain them all and sit with devotion to me. Having brought the senses under control, his wisdom is steady.
>
> When a man constantly thinks about objects, attachment for those objects arises. From attachment is born desire, and from desire is born anger. From anger comes delusion, from delusion comes loss of memory, from loss of memory comes destruction of intellect, and once the intellect is destroyed, he perishes.
>
> But, the one whose mind and senses are under control, is devoid of attraction or revulsion. He moves around objects and gains the state of tranquility.
>
> Having gained tranquility, all of his sorrows are destroyed. His mind is joyful and his intellect soon becomes steady. *Bhagavad Gita*, 2:60-65

Krishna mentions that desire becomes anger. This is more than having a fit of rage with steam coming out of one's ears. It also means frustration and self-pity. These are all distressing conditions that swirl around in our minds like a cyclone when our desires are not fulfilled.

Amma comments on the sweetness of devotion compared to the objects of the world:

> Hearing the song, the brahmacharins who were watching from a distance slowly gathered around the Mother. As She sang, tears of bliss and devotion rolled down Her cheeks. When the song was over, in a semiconscious mood, the Mother slowly sat down and remained still for a while. Then, turning to the brahmacharins, Mother softly said, "Children, the sweetness of devotion is incomparable. Once you taste it, you will never enjoy tasting the objects of the world. Amma, *Awaken Children*, vol. 1

Again more clarity from Amma:

> There is a proverb in Malayalam, "You want to get something sitting on a higher elevation, but you do not want to let go of the thing kept in your armpit." This thing kept in your armpit represents the objects of the world. You are tightly embracing them. If you want to obtain something on a higher level, i.e., eternal happiness, the only thing that you have to do is to loosen your arm a little, and it (the objects of the world) will fall away. But you want both; you want to keep the pleasures of the world and also have spiritual bliss. No, that is impossible. Therefore, slowly let the worldly pleasures fall off

your bosom. Lift your hands and arms fully and the thing under your arm will fall down and you will have the object above. Amma, *Awaken Children*, vol. 3

To cry for God is to gain the highest. Anyway, crying for God is far superior than crying for trivial and fleeting worldly pleasures. The happiness which we get from the objects of the world lasts only for a few seconds; whereas, the happiness experienced from God and the thought of Him is everlasting. Amma, *Awaken Children*, vol. 3

And a comment from Neem Karoli Baba:

If you want to see God, kill desires. Desires are in the mind. When you have a desire for something, don't act on it and it will go away. If you desire to drink this cup of tea, don't, and the desire for it will fall away. - Neem Karoli Baba

From the Bible:

Dear children, keep away from anything that might take God's place in your hearts. *1 John, 5:21,* TLB

Sutra 36 – Unceasing adoration

And by immersing oneself in unceasing adoration of the Beloved.

avyavrttabhajanat

avyavrtta-unceasing; *bhajanat*-worship

We all know that whatever has a beginning must also have an end. How, then, do we reconcile Narada's statement that at some point there is a beginning for an adoration that does not end?

Not having love or adoration is like ignorance. Love is the substratum of the universe. Every atom was created by the Lord as an act of love. Therefore, love and adoration were always present but we were not aware of it. This is because we were lacking in awareness. Once one becomes aware of love and the Beloved it is eternally there because the nature of love and our Beloved is without beginning or end.

By analogy, one might have no knowledge of computers but once the knowledge is gained it doesn't go away. Ignorance has no beginning but has an end. Our adoration has a beginning but has no end.

Amma explains how to do this:

> Devotee: Mother, how can those who are involved in worldly affairs sustain devotion?

Mother: Children, remember God while doing actions. (Mother points to a man who is leading ducks through the backwaters.) There is hardly any room in the boat even to keep his legs properly. It is such a small boat. Standing in the boat, he will row with a long oar and lead the ducks as well. Making noise by slapping the oar on the water, the man will guide the ducks if they stray. At intervals, he will smoke a cigarette. He will scoop out any water entering the boat with his feet. He will also converse with the people standing on the bank. Even while doing all these things, his mind will always be on the boat. If his attention wavers even for a moment, losing his balance, the boat will capsize and he will fall in. Children, like this we should live in this world. Whatever work we are doing, our mind should be centered on God. This is easily possible through practice. Amma, *Awaken Children*, vol. 1

Amma herself is a perfect example of continuous love. The view she offers here is that of the Beloved. This is the view of one who is an incarnation of the Divine. This is how God sees all the beings in the cosmos.

A continuous stream of love flows from me towards all beings in the cosmos. That is Mother's inborn nature. Amma, *Awaken Children*, vol. 1

Sutra 37 – Listening and singing about God

Love for God will come like a consuming fire while living in the world, listening to stories of the Beloved or singing the Lord's praises.

loke 'pi bhagavad-guna-sravana-kirtanat

loke-in the world; *api*-even; *bhagavat*-of the Lord; *guna*-qualities; *sravana*-listening; *kirtanat*-singing

The imagery in this sutra is so potent – to be consumed in a fire of love. For the bhakta this is such an apt description. Once the spark becomes a flame, even if small, the bhakta knows there is no turning back. From then on one is increasingly interested in fanning this flame and throwing the fuel of worship onto it as though one was throwing the impurities of mortal existence into the fires of eternity. There is no bliss, no satisfaction greater than this. Then the bhakta's abiding wish is that others could also swim in the ocean of cosmic bliss.

Narada advises us to sing to God with all our heart, mind and soul, to read stories about the Lord and to talk with others about the Beloved. We will then be able to step into the roaring fire of unfathomable love even while living in the world.

Hafiz was a 14th century Sufi mystic and poet who often used "wine" and "drunkenness" as a metaphor for the bliss of God intoxication.

NO GUARANTEES

These days the only friend that is faultless
Is a bottle of red wine and a book of poems.
Wherever you are going, go alone, for the road
    to enlightenment is very narrow and full of curves.
And take your wineglass with you,
    for there are no guarantees.

I am not the only writer
    that is worried about having a job.
Knowledge without experience is the "wise man's" fate.

In this noisy street, the voice of reason says:
The world and all its possessions is not security.

Let me tell you an old story: the face of an old camel,
destined by Fate to be black, cannot become white
    from washing and cleaning.

Everything you see around you will one day disappear,
Except Love, which lasts forever.

I had great hopes that, with my heart,
    I would unite with You.
But along the Road of Life,
    death lurks like highway robbery.

I say hold on to the Moon-Faced One's hair,
   and don't tell a soul!

For the effect of Saturn and the stars,
   is agony and good luck.
No one will ever see Hafiz sober, never.

He is drunk on the wine of endless Eternity, and keeps
asking for more!

[Hafiz, *Drunk on the Wine of the Beloved - 100 Poems of
Hafiz*, translated by Thomas Rain Crowe, Shambala
Publications, Inc.]

I live my life in a widening circle
That reaches out across the world.
I may not ever complete the last one,
But I give myself to it.

I circle around God, that primordial tower.
I have been circling for thousands of years,
And I still don't know: am I a falcon,
A storm, or a great song?

Rainer Maria Rilke, *Rilke's Book of Hours: Love Poems to God*

Sutra 38 – By the grace of Mahatmas

But mainly by the grace of God-realized Mahatmas and by a drop of the Lord's mercy.

mukhyatastu mahatkrpayaiva bhagavadkrpalesad va

mukhyatah-primarily; *tu*-but; *mahat*-of great souls; *krpaya*-by the grace; *eva*-only; *bhagavad*-the Lord; *krpa*-mercy; *lesat*-small amount; *va*-or

Narada now brings us to the most important, most effective means for stepping into the fire of devotion; for getting pure love for the Beloved. This sutra and the next three are about this.

While devotion comes by singing the glories of the Lord and reading and talking about our beloved as stated in the previous sutra, Narada makes it clear in this sutra that devotion is gotten *mostly* by the grace of a God realized soul – a mahatma (who is one with God). Therefore, a spiritual aspirant should regard the company of such beings as the highest pinnacle of good fortune.

There are some who teach that a guru is not needed because the guru is within us. While this is ultimately true, our hearts are currently lifeless chunks of coal offering no light whatsoever and our minds are confused cyclones filled with the debris of countless delusions, illusions and fantasies. We don't hear the Divine because our minds have too much static. We are not capable of listening to the guru within. We mistake the voices in our head for God.

129

If one wishes to learn carpentry, guitar or brain surgery, one will find a teacher. How much more is this true regarding the spiritual path which is the subtlest of all – teeming with traps of pride and pits of delusion and alligators of woeful advice waiting to swallow us. People who say no guru is needed are those with big egos that are unable to bow down or submit to anyone or anything. Ironically, God realization is about bowing down, submitting and surrendering.

If a guru is truly God realized or Self-realized, they will no longer have an individual ego. It will have been burnt up. What is operating in a satguru is the Cosmic Mind that pervades all of existence. The force of their reality, which is beyond mere conviction and in the realm of infinite knowing, radiates out from them like a blazing sun. They see everyone as their own Self. Everyone is contained in the infinite space of their primordial awareness. When their gaze falls upon us, we are swept up in the satguru's Truth like a leaf is swept away in a waterfall. For this reason, a guru in the flesh is worth a thousand guru's who have since left their body.

Because we are unable to understand the "guru within" that same guru that is within us projects a body and a mind outside of us to direct us on the inward journey. The purpose of this is to eventually connect with the inner guru.

Some people, upon encountering such a soul, experience unexpected tears of joy – sobbing. Some of us don't feel anything at first but we have been caught in the Tiger's jaws and just don't realize it. Our innocent faith will be like a succulent flower that calls to the honey bee of the Divine. God's grace, which is the same as guru's grace, is most attracted by humility.

HOW COULD IT BE?

Mother of life
Jnanis say there are no others
There is only the Self
Bhaktas say there are no others
There is only God

Mother, these are your two breasts
Which feed the universe
Your elixir of love
Your rapture of gnosis
Your ecstasy of endless being
And your children
Are so in love with you!
How could it be
Any other way?

[From the author's book *Divine Mother of the Universe*]

Sutra 39 – Mahatmas are very rare

However, these great Mahatmas are very rare and so their company is difficult to find. We cannot fathom their being and their presence is infallible.

mahat-sangas tu durlabho 'gamyo 'moghas ca

mahat-great soul; *sangas*-keeping the company of; *tu*-but; *durlabhah*-difficult to obtain; *agamyah*-unfathomable; *amoghah*-infallible; *ca*-also

There are many people who claim to be a guru. Many have good things to say but the ones who have completely merged in the Divine are exceedingly rare. They have reached the place of perfect spontaneity. Avatars, those incarnations of God who are born already perfect, are even more rare. Of those who are a bona fide satguru, most are physically difficult to access. One must have their grace in order to even recognize them.

We can't understand many of their actions because we are not privy to their elevated view. A satguru will be a siddha in possession of yogic powers. They will know our every thought as well as what we do and they will see our past lives. This is important because they will recommend a practice that is in keeping with our practice from past lives. They will know when pride has us in its talons. Their every word and action will emanate perfection and should be consumed by the aspirant's eyes and ears. Everything they do is controlled by the Beloved. These beings are very rare and are a great blessing to humanity.

The literary epic the *Ramayana* describes activities in the life of Rama who was an actual person who walked the earth - an incarnation of the Divine. Rama tells his brother Lakshman and his wife Sita why even sitting in the presence of these rare souls is such a blessing:

> Rama: These men of mystic powers live far from the world. They perform penance in this wilderness. They don't exhibit their powers in cities or towns. They are very rare beings. We benefit even by their mere presence.

> Sita: How does their mere presence benefit us?

> Rama: Sita, just as from merely sitting in the sun its warmth enters our bodies. Similarly, being in their physical presence the inner light of their spiritual knowledge, their subtly of emotion, permeates our inner core. Without many words they speak profound truths. To reap full benefit of their wisdom we must keep open the doors and windows of our mind and reside at their feet. If we go to them with all the humility of a beggar, and lay open our minds in receptive calm, the pearls garnered by their penance will be given to you without your striving. Lakshman, only rare fortune gives one such opportunities. Even the sight of such great sages is rarely gained.

In the following quote from Amma, she further underscores this truth:

> Spiritual progress that cannot be had through pilgrimages and austerities can be gained in the presence of mahatmas. We may be able to perform austerities for many years. But the presence of mahatmas is much harder to come by. That is why, if we get a chance to be in their presence, we should never throw it away. The benefits that cannot be gained even after performing austerities for 10 years can be gained from just one darshan or one touch of a mahatma. However, we should approach them without arrogance, but with humility and faith. Only then can we benefit from their presence.   - Amma, *Awaken Children*

Here is another quote from Ramana Maharshi echoing the same theme that there is much to be gained simply by sitting in the presence of a satguru.

> God and Guru are in truth not different.

> Just as the prey that has fallen into the jaws of a tiger cannot escape, so those who have come under the glance of the Guru's grace will surely be saved and will never be forsaken; yet one should follow without fail the path shown by the Guru.

Amma sheds light on the compassion of these Mahatmas:

Amma began talking again: "The thought that Her children are not able to feel compassion, that they cannot see themselves in somebody else's place is extremely painful for Mother.

Without love and compassion the world cannot exist. The whole of existence is indebted to the Mahatmas for the love and compassion they have showered on all creation. This creation and all the creatures in it are an expression of compassion. Those who have attained the state of Self-realization do not want to come down. They go beyond. They are in the beyond. They are the beyond.

Beyond means the state of stillness, the state of Oneness. In that state, there is no motion and there is no thinking because there is no mind. To feel compassion and to feel love, a mind or a thought is needed, a sankalpa (a willful resolve) is required. So from the thoughtless state of 'no-mind,' from the motionless state of stillness, Mahatmas come a step down, maybe not one, but several steps down, because of their concern for those who are helpless and groping in darkness. They have never wanted to come down. Why should they when they are one with eternity? Why should they bother about others? Why should consciousness be concerned with the created world? The fact is there are no concerns in that state of Oneness; there are no feelings in that state. There is neither compassion nor lack of compassion. A mind is created to feel compassion, to feel love, and to be concerned about suffering humanity. By Self-will they create a body to express compassion and love. Once compassion arises within, Mahatmas come down to the human plane of consciousness. Why do they do this? What for? Have you ever thought about it? They do that only to create the spirit of love and compassion in you. Amma, *Awaken Children*, vol. 5

Sutra 40 – Sit in the presence of a Mahatma

Only by God's grace is one able to sit in the physical presence of such a one.

labhyate 'pi tat-krypayaiva

labhyate-is gained; *api*-even; *tat*-that (companionship); *krpaya*-by grace; *eva*-only

In most every case, God's grace is something that is earned. You, dear reader, would not be reading this book (or any similar book) if you had not earned merits in previous lives. In Sanskrit, the term for this earned merit is *punya*. Merit is earned by doing good works and doing spiritual practices. Without this merit, which earns God's grace, we would simply have no interest in spirituality and our attention would be totally at the mercy of Maya (the power of cosmic illusion).

Then, to find one's way to the presence of a satguru (a guru who is wholly God realized and one with the Divine) requires a lot of merit. This merit is again required to recognize the satguru. The satguru could be blazing like a physical sun, walking on water and hugging millions of people and most would still not find this worthy of investigation. It is really astonishing how thoroughly powerful Maya is.

To follow are comments by Amma regarding the need for punya (merits) from past lives:

God-Realization can be attained by doing sadhana (spiritual practices) with this body. It is due to the acquired merits in the previous birth that one feels interested to search for God in this birth. Your desire will be fulfilled in this birth itself if your resolve and effort is continued in the same way. The tendency to enjoy sensual pleasures should completely leave the mind.   Amma, *Awaken Children*, vol. 1

Son, even the thought to live for God arises due to the merits accumulated in the previous birth. Such thoughts arise because we have done good deeds. Circumstances also play their role. A person who lives near a workshop from childhood onwards might learn the work which is done there through friendship with workers. A change can occur in one's life owing to association, but merits acquired from the previous birth are needed even for such circumstances to arise. That is why it is said that merits inherited from the previous birth are needed more than anything else.

Another point to be remembered is this: once one comes to a Perfect Master, all one's sins will be washed away by His or Her grace. After that, one should not waste one's time thinking, "Oh, I am a sinner," but rather one should try to assimilate the Guru's teachings. One should not brood over the past but should start on the spiritual path in earnest when real detachment comes.   Amma, *Awaken Children*, vol. 1

Even if a person has not acquired any spiritual merits in previous lifetimes, a Mahatma, out of sheer compassion and love, can shower His grace on him or on whomever He wants. We do not know in what form this grace will come. Amma, *Awaken Children*, vol. 5

Sutra 41 – Grace of God and Mahatmas

Because there is no difference between the grace of God and the grace of these Mahatmas.

tasmims tajjane bhedabhavat

tasmin-in that grace; *tajjane*-arising from the great mahatmas; *bheda*-difference; *abhavat*-due to the absence

One must be a mahatma to see clearly that there is no difference between the grace of God and the grace of these mahatmas. Otherwise we take it on faith due to what we observe or experience. God is only ONE and so there is no "I." For a mahatma this will also be true. To us they appear to act as we do and so we project our own concept of ourselves onto the mahatma.

A mahatma is continuously the silent witness. Words are said and activities occur but the mahatma only watches. God's Cosmic Mind does the talking and acting. Even this is not quite right because we imagine a separate mahatma watching everything.

Jesus said that if we have the faith of a mustard seed we can say to a mountain, "move" and it will move. A mahatma can do these things but they will rarely interfere with the natural order and the play of karmas by using their powers.

Mahatmas are always selfless as is God. They are always giving love as does God. The more love and compassion a mahatma expresses the more intense is the radiance of God in them.

Because a mahatma is not a person but a thinly veiled mask that God wears, the grace of the mahatma and God is the same.

Sutra 42 – Try to get the grace of God!

Try to get the grace of God alone! Try to get the grace of God alone!

tadeva sadhyatam tadeva sadhyatam

tat-that grace; *eva*-only; *sadhyatam*-should be strived for

This is the only sutra where Narada exclaims so emphatically! As students we should ponder this very closely. Really think deeply about it. Maya will put a glaze over our eyes and prevent us from seeing the naked blazing truth of this sutra.

We can spend the next million lifetimes chipping away at our vast mountain range of egoistic notions, habits and concepts that we have accumulated over past uncountable eons and not get very far. Or, we can get the grace of God and be done with it! Get the grace of God and be done with it!

Sri Ramakrishna comments on the grace of God:

> Those who seek God with intense longing see Him, make acquaintance with Him, speak with Him, just in the same manner as I am speaking to you. I am telling you the truth when I say that God can be seen. Who will listen to me and who will believe me?

Can God be found in the Scriptures? After reading the Scriptures, the highest knowledge one can get is about the existence of a God; but God does not appear to him who does not dive below the surface. Until then doubts are not removed and Divine knowledge does not come. You may read thousands of volumes, you may repeat verses and hymns by hundreds, but if you cannot dive into the ocean of Divinity with extreme longing of the soul, you cannot reach God. A scholar may delude the people by his knowledge of the Scriptures and by his book-learning, but through these he will not attain to God. Scriptures, books, sciences, what good will they do? Nothing can be acquired without the Grace of the Lord. Yearn after His Grace, devote your energy to obtaining it and by His Grace you will see Him and He will be glad to speak to you.

Nisargadatta Maharaj comments:

Questioner: Am I permitted to ask you how did you go beyond the mind?

Maharaj: By the grace of my Guru.

Sutra 43 – Avoid worldly people

Abandon the company of worldly seeking persons as one would shun poison.

duhsangam sarvathaiva tyajyah

duhsangam-bad association; *sarvatha*-in every way; *eva*-indeed; *tyajyah*-to be given up

It is the nature of the mind to assume the qualities and vibrations of whatever or whoever it dwells on. As beginners, we will be working hard to keep the mind focused on the Beloved. We are trying to escape the gravity of Maya – the power of cosmic illusion. And we are all beginners up until the time of the final surrender.

Worldliness means to be fascinated with the people and things of the world to the extent that we think they provide us with a source of happiness. Of course, this is delusional and it is a delusion shared by almost every single person on this earth. No lasting happiness will ever come from anything outside of our self. Jesus said the kingdom of God is within us – Luke 17:21

Because of this, we wish to avoid the company of persons who are fixated on getting all the pleasure they can and being as comfortable as possible.

Comments by Yogananda:

> Be always with people who inspire you; surround yourself with people who lift you up. Do not let your resolutions and positive thinking be poisoned by bad company. Even if you cannot find good company to inspire you, you can find it in meditation. The best company you can have is the joy of meditation. - Yogananda

> Many temptations to revert to wrong habits, haphazard thinking, and restlessness beset the beginner-yogi. The delusive force of Maya is powerful and difficult to overcome, especially at first. Thus, those who wish to perfect themselves are urged by the masters to keep in close association with others of similar nature in order to strengthen their right aspirations.

> We become like the people we mingle with, not only through their conversation, but through the silent magnetic vibration that emanates from them. When we come into the range of their magnetism we are affected. - Yogananda

And Ramakrishna:

> Those who are thus caught in the net of the world are the *Baddha*, or bound souls. No one can awaken them. They do not come to their senses even after receiving blow upon blow of misery, sorrow and

indescribable suffering. The camel loves thorny bushes, and although his mouth bleeds when he eats them, still he does not cease to love them dearly and no one can keep him away from them. The bound souls may meet with great grief and misfortune, but after a few days they are just as they were before. The wife may die or become unchaste, the man will marry again; his son may die, he will be extremely sorrowful, but he will soon forget him. The mother of the boy may be overwhelmed with grief for a short time, but in a few days she will once more be concerned for her personal appearance and will deck herself with jewels and finery. Such worldly people may be left paupers after marrying their sons and daughters, yet they will still beget children every year. They may lose their fortune by a lawsuit, but they will again go to the courts. They may not be able to support their children, to educate, feed, clothe, or house them properly, still they will continue to have more. They are like the snake with a musk-rat in its mouth. As the snake cannot swallow the rat because of its strong odor, neither can it throw it out because of its own bent teeth, so these bound souls, *Baddhas*, although they may occasionally feel that the world is unreal, can neither give it up nor can they fix their minds on the Reality of the universe. I once saw a relative of Keshab Chunder Sen, who was quite old, still playing cards as if the time for meditating on God had not come for him.

There is another sign of a *Baddha*, or worldly soul. If you remove him from the world and put him in a better place, he will pine away and die. He will work like a slave to support his family, and he will not hesitate to tell lies, to deceive or to flatter in order to earn his livelihood. He looks upon those who worship God or who meditate on the Lord of the universe as insane. He never finds time or opportunity to think of spiritual subjects. Even at the hour of death he will think and talk of worldly things. Whatever thought is strongest in the minds of worldly people comes out at the time of death. If they become delirious, they rave of nothing but material objects. - *Gospel of Ramakrishna*, translated by Swami Abhedananda

Sutra 44 – Evil company is the cause

Because evil company is the cause of infatuation with pleasure, anger, forgetting spiritual goals, being unable to know right from wrong and the real from the unreal, and complete destruction.

kama-krodha-moha-smrti-brahmsa-buddhi-nasa-sarva-nasa-karanatvat

kama-lust, pleasure seeking; *krodha*-anger; *moha*-delusion, bewilderment; *smrti-brahmsa*-loss of memory of spiritual goal; *buddhi-nasa*-loss of discrimination knowing the real from the unreal; *sarva-nasa*-loss of everything; *karanatvat*-being the cause of

There is no greater force for failure than the influence of others. This can also include movies, books and music. Negative tendencies already exist within our own minds and it is difficult to weed them out even when our environment is perfect. When we associate with persons of worldly or evil inclination, it is like continuing to sow seeds of undesirable traits in the gardens of our minds.

On one hand we are drawn to spirituality. We are beginning to awaken and in the light of our increasing awareness we also see the suffering we endure from the weight of our own ego and the suffering of others due to their egos. We might have had a cosmic experience to further expand our interest. On the other hand, we have spent years enjoying movies. The content of most movies revolve around delusional realities such as stealing, adultery, revenge, violence, pleasure seeking, thinking happiness is going to be found in relationships and so on. The subject matter of most movies are counter to the direction we want to take. Still, the movies are fun and entertaining. Suppose we are doing fairly well at avoiding movies. Then a friend calls and invites us to see a recent release. We say no but the friend doesn't have anyone else to go with and pressures us with very persuasive arguments. It's a science fiction movie and we love Sci Fi! At last we succumb to please our friend and also because we still harbor the desire to see movies.

Persons who have gone through the Alcoholics Anonymous program know this theme very well. If we want to control the addiction that is alcohol, we must avoid keeping the company of those who still indulge. We must never go in a bar. Once one commits to AA, one's list of friends will change dramatically. The pursuit of spirituality requires giving up our worldly interests which provide a source of intoxication just like bottles of wine. We are going to trade all that in on the healthy intoxication of the Divine!

And we have so many addictions! Movies, gossiping, food, sex, traveling, and the list is endless. All of these will make us stupid, blind and ignorant.

A comment from Amma:

We are spending our days in body-consciousness with a heart full of sorrow. What a pity that the devil of desire, which affects us through illusory temptations, kicks us into the dark abyss of Maya (illusion), making us food for the god of Death. If you get caught in the grip of the devil of desire, woe to you! for you will lose your soul. All worries will come to an end if only you give up your desires and keep your hopes in God alone." Amma, *Omkara Divya Porule,* part 4

Sutra 45 – Evil is ripples at first

At first, evil appears as ripples and then waves and soon swells into an all-consuming ocean in which one will surely drown.

tarangita apime sangat samudrayanti

tarangita-forming small waves; *api*-even; *ime*-these; *sangat*-by physical association; *samudrayanti*-become a swelling ocean

A ball that is slowly pushed off the top step of a staircase bounds down the stairs in increasingly greater strides. This is the insidiousness of "evil." We have heard the analogy of a frog that is put into a pot of water and placed on a fire. As the water heats slowly, the frog does not attempt to escape until finally it succumbs. Negative habits and tendencies start small and escalate. This is also true for intoxicants like alcohol. So many lives are destroyed in a pit of misery just like this.

Sutra 46 – Who can cross this ocean?

Who can cross this ocean? Who can cross over this illusion of Maya? Only those who let go of bad company, who keep the company of the Saints and Sages and who are free from the feeling of "I" and "mine."

kastarati kastarati mayam? Yah sangamtyajati yo mahanubhavam sevate nirmamo bhavati

kastarati-who crosses beyond; *Kastarati*-who crosses beyond; *mayam*-the great cosmic illusion; yah-one who; *sangam*-physical association; *tyajati*-abandons; *yah*-one who; *mahanubhavam*-enlightened souls; *sevate*-serves; *nirmamah*-without feeling of "I"; *bhavati*-becomes

> This divine power (Maya) of Mine, consisting of three states of matter or mind, is very difficult to overcome. Only those who surrender unto Me easily cross over this Maya. – Krishna, *Bhagavad Gita*, 7.14

For millions of births we have journeyed from single cell creatures, to plants, insects, fish, birds, animals and finally humans. We have experienced birth and death countless times. This seemingly endless round of births and deaths is Samsara and it is caused by the Lord's power of illusion or creation which is Maya.

The universe could not exist without the divine cosmic power of Maya. Those who worship God also bow to Maya. The world is not rejected but embraced. The bhakta is moved to serve others, animals, plants and the earth. All of this is the glory of God's infinite play (leela in Sanskrit). Utmost respect and reverence is given to both animate and inanimate beings as well as subtle beings who are not incorporated in a physical body.

By the grace of the Beloved, some people develop a desire to step out of the cycle of birth and death. For them, the Lord has provided much help and instruction. Their habitual immersion in the illusion of Maya will, by its very nature, pull them back into the dream of worldly existence and the pursuit of personal pleasures. Therefore, it is necessary to understand the nature of Maya and how to wake up.

Krishna tells us in the quote from the *Bhagavad Gita* previously, that the easiest way to cross over the ocean of Samsara is to practice love for the Lord – to be a devoted bhakta. It can be Krishna, or Jesus, or the Divine Mother, or Divine Light or any aspect of the Beloved. It is the love itself that is most important.

Sutra 47 – Seek solitude; eliminate desire and fear

One who seeks solitude, serves the Great Ones, who eliminates desire and fear which are the chains of the world, who is no longer affected by the three qualities of nature, and who abandons the idea that happiness is dependent on things outside of oneself.

yo viviktasthanam sevate yo loka-bandha munmulayati
nistraigunyo bhavati yogaksemam tyajati

yah-one who; *viviktasthanam*-seclusion; *sevata*-is given to; *yah*-one who; *loka*-mundane world; *bhandam*-bondage; *munmulayati*-eliminates; *nistraigunyo*-liberated from the three qualities of Nature; *bhavati*-becomes; *yah*-who; *yogaksemam*-desire for gaining security from things of the world; *tyajati*-abandons, gives up

Narada continues to give advice for crossing the Great Ocean. As one approaches the fiery heart of the Beloved, the desire for the company of others or to mingle in the throbbing masses of humanity diminish. This is replaced with a fascination for the transcendental beauty and bliss of the Divine which is perceived as a blazing glory in the center of one's own being.

If one knows a God realized soul then one can serve this person. Jesus asked us to serve the poor and also said that whatsoever we do to the least of persons we also do to him. There are so many ways.

Desire and fear are the banks of the river between which the fantasy of our separate egocentric existence flows. The ego is a high maintenance contraption that is held together with the bubble gum and bailing wire of numberless identities. That which supports and facilitates these identities creates desire and that which diminishes or fades these identities produces fear. This is a preponderous burden we have carried for so long we have forgotten we are carrying it.

The three qualities of Nature or *gunas*, are the Vedic version of yin and yang except there are three primal qualities instead of two that are required to compose the universe. The three gunas are *tamas*, *rajas* and *sattvas*. Tamas is ignorance, darkness, lethargy. Rajas is passion, activity, vigor. Sattvas is peaceful equilibrium.

If we are fortunate, we start to catch on. Happiness is, by and large, not going to result from anything outside of us. The good news is that there is a much better happiness than the fleeting sniffs of happy moments that result from things in the world, places or relationships. There is a happiness that never goes away and it is to this that Narada directs us. This happiness is to be found within our own being at the place where all beings emanate from the sun behind all suns.

> We are caught in the illusion that we will get happiness from the world. Then we madly run here and there craving to acquire it. Having unfulfilled desires, frustration and anger results. Without

discriminating between the necessary and the unnecessary, we do things as we like. Can we say that this is life?   Amma, *Awaken Children*, vol. 1

OH SMALL SELF,
YOU ARE A SPARKLING FISH

Oh small self, you are a sparkling fish
   at play in the ocean of consciousness
and your life is swiftly coming to its end.
Death will skim above you and throw its sharp net.
You will not be protected by your watery world,
for selfish actions have kept you in the shallows.

The fisherman's net will surround you suddenly.
Why do you remain
   so near the surface of relative existence
   where Death is granted its fishing grounds?
Yet there is still time.
Leave the dangerous shoreline, mundane mind,
and plunge into silent profundity,
the black waters of Mother Kali's mystery.

[*Mother of the Universe,* poetry of Ramprasad,
translated by Lex Hixon, Quest Books]

Sutra 48 – Abandon the need for compensation

He who abandons expectation for the fruit or reward of one's activities, and is free from the pairs of opposites such as joy and sorrow, gain and loss and pain and pleasure.

yah karmaphalam tyajati karmani sannyasyati tato nirvandvo bhavati

yah-one who; *karmaphalam*-the fruit of one's efforts; *tyajati*-renounces; *karmani*-activities; *sannyasyati*-resigns; *tatah*-and so; *nirvandvo*-free from the pairs of opposites; *bhavati*-becomes

Krishna speaks:

> Arjuna, know that the mode of passion is characterized by intense craving for sense gratification, and is the source of material desire and attachment. The mode of passion binds the living entity by attachment to the fruits of work. Krishna, *Bhagavad Gita*, 14.07

> Lord Krishna said: The sages define renunciation as abstaining from all work for personal profit. The wise define sacrifice as the sacrifice of, and the freedom from, the selfish attachment to the fruits of all work. Krishna, *Bhagavad Gita*, 18.02

It is difficult to renounce attachment to the fruit of all work. This is especially true if one goes to a job that is unpleasant

157

and gets paid a wage for each hour that is worked. The joy of getting a paycheck so we can pay our past due electric bill is irrefutable. If one has a nice job in the health care profession, it is a little easier to think of one's work as being for the benefit of others. But try we must regardless of the circumstances. Our goal is to abandon all self-centered habits. Attachment to the fruit of our efforts looms large on the horizon of the spiritual path. Eventually we want to be completely dependent on the Beloved for our well-being. Every act we perform is an act of love offered to our Beloved. We are going to replace one habitual way of thinking (what's in it for me) with another (I give this to You).

Being free from the pairs of opposites is known as equanimity. All the same through praise and blame. The Lord giveth and the Lord taketh away. What goes around comes around. Here today and gone tomorrow. What goes up must come down. She loves me; she loves me not. The universe could not exist without pairs of opposites. Light/dark, big/little, inside/outside, gain/loss, hard/soft, good/bad, birth/death, centrifugal/centripetal, male/female, yin/yang.

Pondering this truth will begin to release us from its grip. We commonly desire one or fear another of these opposites. We desire to gain money and we fear loss of money. We desire a life mate or we fear they will leave us. We desire a body and we fear death. All desires and all fears revolve around the ego-centered view of "what's in it for me?" This agitates the mind to no end and leaves no room to love our Beloved. Love and devotion for the Lord is the opposite direction of what's-in-it-for-me.

THE HAND OF THE BELOVED

The hand of the Beloved is silent
Leading us into our heart
So that love can bloom
In the garden of our devotion
Where the soft rain of bliss
Falls like drops of golden light
Seeking the root of our being

Sutra 49 – Feel unbroken love for God

And renouncing even the scriptures one is able to feel unbroken love for God.

yo vedan api sannyasyati kevalam avicchinnanuragam labhate

yah-who; *vedan*-scriptures (Vedas); *api*-even; *sannyasyati*-renounces; *kevalam*-complete; *avicchinna*-unceasing; *anuragam*-intense devotion; *labhate*-obtains

For one who has arrived at unceasing love for God, scriptures are irrelevant. Once the fireworks have ignited, a lighter is no longer necessary.

> Question: How should one maintain the constant remembrance of God?

> Amma: Children, Mother knows that it is difficult for you who live in the midst of material pleasures and with family ties, to remember God constantly. But when you become aware that you are not remembering Him, immediately repent, "O Lord, I have forgotten you for this much time. I have forgotten to chant Your Divine Name for this length of time. O Lord, please forgive me. Please bestow upon me the mental strength to cherish Your Form within and Your Name on my lips constantly and incessantly. O Lord, please do not let me waste time like this. Let the desire to behold Thy Form burn within me." Having repented and prayed thus,

immediately start repeating the mantra. Again you might forget it. Don't worry, go on applying the same technique of repentance and prayer whenever you realize that you have not been chanting the mantra for a long time. Slowly in due course, you will develop the power to remember Him incessantly. Amma, *Awaken Children*, vol. 3

Ramakrishna:

A man brought a bottle of wine; I went to touch it but could not.

Disciple: Why, Bhagavan?

When Divine bliss is attained, one becomes intoxicated with it, he does not need to drink wine. When I see the feet of my Divine Mother, I feel as intoxicated as if I had drunk five bottles of wine. In this state one cannot eat anything and everything. *Gospel of Ramakrishna*, translated by Swami Abhedananda

Sutra 50 – One crosses the ocean of Samsara

Verily one crosses; he crosses this ocean of limitation and helps all the world to cross over.

sa tarati sa tarati sa lokamstarayati

sah-he; *tarati*-crosses beyond; *sa*- he; *tarati*- crosses beyond; *sa*- he; *lokan*-all the world; *tarayati*-helps to cross

For most of us, walking through our day to day lives is a walk through a lot of separate things and people – an ocean of things, plants, creatures and people. We perceive ourselves as being an individual person who is sitting up in the bridge of the brain – like Captain Kirk would sit in the command chair on the bridge of the USS Enterprise.

From there we perceive that we are pulling levers to move limbs and peering out through the observation windows of the eyes and tracking sound waves with the radar of our ears. Our body/spacecraft is interacting with so many things "out there."

The truth is we are what is aware. What we are is awareness itself. When this is pondered deeply enough, the mind begins to identify with awareness and, when that occurs, the body and all of the people and objects of the world are seen as occurring within our awareness – within our own Self. It's not exactly within because that would imply that awareness is like a box that has six sides of containment. Awareness is limitless space. Nonetheless, all the universe, including our own body, occurs in this

162

awareness – it is actually in us. Our own Self, as pure, formless, limitless, spacious awareness enfolds all of the people and things much like we might imagine a holographic stage into which is projected a great play.

All of the comings and goings of the universe are seen as God. The light of a thousand suns that is behind every atom and every being is God. God is this universal awareness and as we realize we are enfolded in That, the ego recedes like a train disappearing into the distant night. When our love flows to the Beloved without interruption, this is the merging. We have crossed over the ocean of separate things and people and arrived at the magnificent light and love of infinite being. Having done this, we may choose to help others who are struggling with the heavy weight of ego-centered delusions. We are in a position to help them cross over as well.

Sutra 51 – Essential nature of love

The essential nature of this love between the lover and the Beloved can never be put into words or thoughts.

anivacaniyam prema-svarupam

anivacaniyam-without description; *prema*-love; *svarupam*-essential essence

SWEPT AWAY

Mother of Light
Your children gaze at you
Stupefied and dumbfounded
We have not one root left
To bind the soil
Of our worldly existence

With hair standing on end
We are burrowing through the shadows
That once hid your radiant light
And we have discovered our innocence
In the naked sun dance
Of your mysterious eternity

We have tasted
The sweet gossamer ambrosia
Of your intoxicating bliss
That is ever exploding
In showers of mind-dissolving light and love
Binding aimless wandering galaxies

To every flickering flame
Of courageous prayer

Now our tongues taste only sawdust
Our eyes see only empty streets
Our ears are deaf to all else
But your cascading waterfall
Of Love

Your children have reached
The point of no return
Having fallen
So deeply in love with you
We are swept away
In the river
Of your warm embrace

[From the author's book *Divine Mother of the Universe*]

The rewards of life and devotion to God are love
and inner rapture, and the capacity to receive the
light of God.   Rumi

Sutra 52 – Like a person who is mute

Like a person who is mute cannot describe what he tastes.

mukasvadanavat

muka-of a mute; *asvadana*-tasting; *vat*-like

Even a person who can talk cannot describe what he tastes. Using words to describe the rapture of God's bliss is like trying to play Beethoven's Ninth Symphony by banging two rocks together. The best that one can do is describe how one found the oasis of the Heart.

Amma, from *Awaken Children*, vol. 1:

The Mother stopped talking and started singing:

> Come, O Mother, Who art the
> Enchantress of the mind.
> Give me, O Ambika, Thy Vision.
> Let Thy Form shine
> In the lotus of my heart.
>
> When will dawn that blessed day
> When my heart will become full of
> Devotion to Thee?
> Satiated with the repetition of Thy

Name, when will blissful tears flow
From my eyes?

The Holy Mother went into samadhi. She shed tears of bliss. Regaining Her consciousness, the Mother said, "Son, the taste of devotion is something unique."

Mother's hug
Smell of roses
River overflowing

Sutra 53 – In some rare persons

In some rare persons, this divine love is expressed with great brilliance like the sun radiates heat and light.

prakasyate kvapi patre

prakasyate-it is shown; *kva api*-occasionally, rarely; *patre*-to a worthy recipient

Occasionally mahabhaktas – great lovers of God – incarnate and we are given direct evidence for the existence of the intensely blissful states of devotion one feels for the Beloved. The bhakta immersed in this river feels their own love going to the Beloved and also love coming back from the Beloved. There is an intimate communion that is beyond describing. Often these great lovers will lose consciousness as their minds rise up like a beach ball that has been held underwater and then released.

For the rest of us, even a small spark of the bliss they experience is more than satisfying.

From the *Gospel of Ramakrishna*, translated by Swami Abhedananda:

> There was a deep silence at the close of this song, which had been listened to with rapt attention. Everyone was moved. At the end of this song the Bhagavan was once more found to be in that indescribable state of *Samadhi*. His sweet divine voice became still. His eyes remained fixed and

steadfast. But his spiritual eye was feasting on the beatific Vision of the Divine Glory! There was left just enough of self-consciousness to bring the soul face to face with the Divine Mother. This blessed Vision the Bhagavan enjoyed for a long time. His face was radiant with celestial light and expressed by sweet smiles the unbounded happiness which He was enjoying within Himself, and in His semiconscious state He uttered these words:

Bhakti, or devotion, means whole-hearted love for the Lord. The Absolute Brahman is called "Divine Mother" by the Psalmist. Prasad asks his mind to understand it by hints; He who is described in the Vedas as the Absolute Brahman is my Divine Mother; I am praying to Her.

Sutra 54 – This love is subtle, sublime bliss

This love is felt as an exquisitely subtle and sublime bliss beyond the conditions of Nature, desireless, boundless and expanding moment by moment into the infinite.

guna-rahitam kamana-rahitam pratiksana-vardhamanam avicchinam suksma-taram anubhava-rupam

guna-rahitam-devoid of material conditions; *kamana-rahitam*-devoid of worldly desires; *pratiksana*-ever enduring; *vardhamanam*-expanding; *avicchinam*-boundless; *suksma-taram*-sublimely subtle; *anubhava-rupam*-of the nature of immanent experience

Divine love is a river that flows. Where it is from and where it is going no one can say. This is its great mystery! Not having a beginning and an end, we are unable to say there is any reason or goal to love. A goal or purpose would imply and end and there is no end. Because love has no purpose, it is desireless.

Love is empty like space and so it is boundless – having no boundaries. Moment by moment love is expanding which we observe as the universe and all the subtle worlds expanding for eternity. After each successive dissolution, the universe is reborn and it will be bigger than the last incarnation. This limitless expansion is a reflection of the boundless nature of love.

Love does not revolve in the realm of the three gunas or qualities of the physical universe (tamas, rajas and sattva). It is the other way around – the qualities of the universe were created out of love and revolve in love.

There is nothing more sublime than a mystery that one realizes can never be answered. One does not really know this until it is experienced directly. It is an experience of looking directly into eternity.

As it is with love, we can look at existence itself and ask why does anything at all exist? Why not nothing? And yet it is. The one thing we can't deny is our own existence. This mystery will never be solved. There is something eternally fresh and new and exhilarating in this fact.

White cranes flying
Against dark rain clouds
Even the dogs stop barking

Sutra 55 – He thinks of his beloved alone

Abiding in that fiery love for the Beloved, one sees love everywhere, hears love everywhere, speaks only of his Beloved and thinks of his Beloved alone.

tat prapya tadevavalokayati tadeva srnoti tadeva bhasayati tadeva cintayati

tat-that (sublime bliss of love per sutra 54); *prapya*-having attained; *tadeva*-the Beloved alone; *avalokayati*-one sees; *tadeva*-the Beloved alone; *srnoti*-one hears about; *tadeva*-the Beloved alone; *bhasayati*-one speaks about; *tadeva*-the Beloved alone; *cintayati*-one thinks about

Everything is alive! It's all alive! It's all God! This is how the bhakta perceives the world after realizing God. It is easy to see the vegetable and animal kingdom as being alive, but now the bhakta sees that rocks are alive as are rivers, mountains, stars, valleys, sky, clouds and, in fact, the entire universe is the body of the Beloved. However, it doesn't stop here. Words are alive, each number is alive and has its own personality, the planets are alive and musical instruments are incarnations of the goddess Saraswati. The primal dualities of yin and yang are living conscious beings who pervade all of existence. There are seven principalities represented by the seven colors of the rainbow and the seven chakras and the seven seals on the Book of Life in the Bible. These are living beings that interpenetrate the cosmos and further multiplicity is derived from them. The three gunas are all living beings.

All of it is the Beloved! This is what the lover and knower of God experiences.

There is an interesting story. Amma had just arrived at the home of the persons hosting Amma and her troupe of compassionateers in Santa Fe, New Mexico. Pulling up to the front of the house everyone got out. Some started around the front of the car and Amma started with them and then reversed course going around the back of the car. She explained that she felt it was disrespectful to walk in front of the face of the car. To Amma the car was alive.

Sutra 56 – According to the qualities of each

There are three types of secondary devotion and, according to the qualities or conditions of each person, this love manifests itself differently.

gauni tridha gunabhedad artadibhedad va

gauni-secondary; *tridha*-threefold; *guna*-of the three qualities of Nature; *bhedad*-according to differentiation; *artadi*-of the one who is disturbed; *bhedad*-according to differentiation; *va*-or

Ramakrishna comments in the *Gospel of Ramakrishna*, translated by Swami Abhedananda:

> People's characters can be divided into three classes,—*Tamas*, *Rajas* and *Sattwa*. Those who belong to the first class are egotistic; they sleep too much, eat too much, and passion and anger prevail in them. Those who belong to the second class are too much attached to work. They love nice, well-fitting clothes and are very neat; they care for a luxurious, richly furnished house; when they sit and worship God, they love to wear costly garments; when they give anything to charity they parade it. Those who belong to the third class are very quiet, peaceful, unostentatious; they are not particular about their dress, they lead a simple life and earn a modest living, because their needs are small; they do not flatter for selfish ends; their dwelling is

modest; they do not worry about their children's dress; they are not anxious for fame, nor do they care for the admiration or adulation of others; they worship God, give charity and meditate silently and in secret. This Sattwa quality is the last step of the ladder which leads to the roof of Divinity. A person reaching this state does not have to wait long for God-consciousness.

A devotee endowed with tamas is prone to proclaiming that his way is the only way. Religious wars are the activity of tamas. A tamasic person is narrow minded and can kill in the name of his religion. His devotion has a selfish motive in wanting to receive wealth, food, sensual pleasure, children and favorable resolution to problems.

A devotee endowed with rajas is prone to pomp and ceremony. He will display religious artifacts prominently on his person for show and make certain all know when he performs an act of charity. These persons will prefer colorful robes and vestments for religious activities. He is possessed of intellectual curiosity and plows through books on philosophy and religion.

A devotee endowed with sattva will be peaceful and indrawn neither forcing a point of view nor displaying his religiosity with pride. They are concerned with relieving the pain and suffering of others and look upon God as a force of good.

Sutra 57 – Each is progressively more noble

Each succeeding type of devotion is more noble than the one before it.

uttarasmad uttarasmat purvapurva sreyaya bhavati

uttarasmad uttarasmat-than each one following; *purva-purvah*-each one before; *sreyaya bhavati*-is to be considered more noble

Narada presents these three types of devotion as legitimate stepping stones on the path to prema-bhakti which is the highest transcendental form of love for the Divine. In Narada's view some devotion is better than no devotion and each will eventually lead to the next level of awareness.

Tamasic devotion is the lowest level followed by rajasic and then sattvic devotion. Sattvic devotion is the final spring board leading to union with the Beloved. The underlying emotional current for tamasic devotion is selfishness; for rajasic devotion it is passion; for sattvic devotion it is compassion.

MY SWEET LORD

My sweet Lord
Hm, my Lord
Hm, my Lord
I really want to see you
Really want to be with you
Really want to see you Lord
But it takes so long, my Lord
My sweet Lord
Hm, my Lord
Hm, my Lord
I really want to know you
Really want to go with you
Really want to show you Lord
That it won't take long, my Lord (hallelujah)

[Lyrics from the song *My Sweet Lord* by George Harrison on the album *All Things Must Pass*]

177

Sutra 58 – Path of devotion is the most direct

The path of devotion is the simplest most direct way to salvation.

anyasmat saulabhyam bhaktau

anyasmat-than any others; *saulabhyam*-easier to attain, readily available; *bhaktau*-in (the path of) devotion

Hafiz, the 14th century Sufi poet comments:

WHY CARRY?

Hafiz,
Why carry a whole load of books upon your back
Climbing this mountain, when tonight,
Just a few thoughts of God
Will light the holy fire.

Each person, no matter what temperament, can find a place on the devotional path. Narada has discussed this in the previous two sutras. No other path is so accommodating to such a large swath of humanity.

God is love and everyone has the capacity to love. Devotion begins in the heart of the Beloved and ends there and so it is the most direct path. No other path can say this. There are no complicated techniques – it is very simple. Nothing is as powerful, as healing and as transforming as love.

Yogananda:

> Devotion is the secret key, for God cannot resist the outpourings of great love from a true devotee's heart.

God will not be moved nearly so much by our yoga postures, self-inquiry, meditations and chakra clearings – if at all. God immediately will turn to us and come running when we pour out our sincere love and longing to Him.

Because love is available to us all and there is nothing complicated about it and because God runs toward the sincere devotee – all of this conspires to make the path of devotion the simplest, easiest and most direct path to the Divine.

> He cannot be perceived by the senses or grasped by the mind. By contemplating Him, peace comes. He Himself draws you towards Him.
>
> - Sri Anandamayi Ma

Sutra 59 – The proof is self-evident

The proof of this is self-evident requiring no other proof.

pramanantarasyanapeksatvat svayam pramanatvat

praman-means of valid knowing; *antarasya*-another; *anapeksatvat*-because of not having dependence on; *svayam*-all on its own; *pramanatvat*-being itself the authority

In the same way that love is its own reward and that it is both the path and the goal, so too, love is its own proof. The experience of love and bliss from the very beginning of this path is all the proof that is necessary. This is one of the reasons the path of bhakti is supreme.

There is no place for the intellect or reason in the presence of love. When one enters the heart, the intellect will have to be left on the shoe rack. What can be said about love? There is no describing it and there are no formulae to ponder. For this reason, devotion is the silent path.

For those with intellectual momentum, the paths of jnana yoga and raja yoga provide more initial intellectual satisfaction than the path of devotion. With both of these paths the practitioner is concerned with oneself primarily and how to bring oneself into the Self. In contrast, the lover of God is not concerned about his or her fate or spiritual development. The interest is solely in the Beloved. The bhakta wholly surrenders to the Lord and accepts whatever progress is or is not made as the will of the Beloved. It is just not a concern. According to Narada, realizing God and having love for God is the highest peak. That is love. All paths must eventually end in Love. That is the highest point of all spiritual endeavor.

The jnani does not find proof until the end when Self-realization dawns. Through love, the bhakta will know the Self (sat) of the jnanis and consciousness (chit) of the Raja yogis automatically.

> Mother showed the tip of one of Her fingers. "In front of bhakti (devotion for God), mukti (liberation from the cycle of birth and death) is no more than this." Amma, *Eternal Wisdom*, vol. 2

While practitioners of other paths labor over ever increasing complexities in technique the bhakta simply lifts his arms and cries out to the Lord. The Lord cannot resist the love and the innocence of the bhakta. The bhakta realizes that he is wholly incapable of salvation regardless of the path and that his only option is surrender.

Ramakrishna comments on this:

> To see God one must love Him with the whole heart and soul. One must make one's prayers reach the Divine Mother. Absolute self-resignation to the will of the Divine Mother is the surest way to God-vision. As the kitten resigns itself to the will of its mother, so a devotee shall resign himself to the will

of the Divine Mother. The kitten knows nothing more than to cry "Mew, mew," and the mother-cat may keep her young one on the bare floor of the kitchen or on the downy bed of the householder. The kitten is always contented. Similarly, the true devotee should always cry unto the Divine Mother and be contented with whatever She wishes to do with him.

LOVE IS FEARLESS

Love is fearless
It will play in the dark
It calls us to join
Even though we don't answer
Love is in no hurry
It sees the emptiness in our heart
And longs to fill it
If it were otherwise
It wouldn't be love

Sutra 60 – Its nature is peace and bliss

Because its nature is peace and perfect bliss.

shanti-rupat paramananda-rupac ca

shanti-peace; *rupat*-the nature of it being; *param*-utmost; *ananda*-bliss, joy; *rupac*-the nature of it being; *ca*-and

Narada continues to expound on the nature of love. In the previous sutra he tells us that love is more noble because it is its own proof and now he presents the idea that contained within it is peace of mind and perfect bliss. These are qualities of love in the same way that heat and light are qualities of fire.

By stepping into the river of devotional love, the mind becomes fixed on the beloved replacing all other thoughts. This stillness is profound peace. Bliss rises to the surface. This happens automatically with no effort other than the cultivation of our love.

> Crying to God for five minutes is equal to one hour of meditation. Amma, *Awaken Children*, vol. 2

Sutra 61 – All anxiety is gone

There is no anxiety because everything has been surrendered to the Lord.

Lokahanau cinta na karya niveditatmalokavedatvat

Lokahanau – worldly losses or calamities; *cinta* – anxiety; *na* – not; *karya* – duty; *niveditatma* – giving of oneself; *lokavedatvat* – of traditional duties in the world

Amma comments on this:

> Surrender all that we have to Bhagavan (the Lord). We will go to the railway station when we travel, carrying heavy loads. After getting into the train, we do not continue to carry the luggage on our head. Having unloaded it, we comfortably sit in our seat, don't we? Once faith in God arises, then surrender everything at His Feet. We should live with the attitude that He will protect us. Everything is His, nothing is mine, He will take care of everything. We have to think this way.   Amma, *Awaken Children*, vol. 1

Of course it takes some practice to reorient the mind that is accustomed to living in its usual lair of fear. Further complicating this, the ego becomes identified with our problems, concerns and stresses. It says, "I am a poor person" or "I am a vulnerable person." It feels that if it is not afraid of these things thus giving due respect, it will

184

weaken its foundation leading to eventual non-existence. The ego adopts these identities as part of the facade it builds to make itself seem real. Each identity is a paper mache strip that is carefully placed over the wire mesh frame of our imagined persona.

We first become aware of these machinations in the mind and begin watching for them. When the fear occurs, we talk to our Beloved and offer them to Him. We contemplate the fact that we have surrendered everything to the Lord and whatever happens we will accept. Doing so is like taking an antidote to counteract the poison of fear and worry.

GARLAND OF POEMS

My Beloved Divine Mother
I place this garland of poems around your neck
    Each simply says "I love you"

Now I bow before you
   like a blade of grass bent to the ground
   in the hurricane wind of your compassion

I am praying
with folded hands
    that I might become small enough
      to sit on your lap
        and be held in your arms
          listening to your lamp of rainbow light
            singing in the empty space of eternity

Sutra 62 – Continue social customs

Until devotion ripens, one should continue social customs and ceremonies with only the fruits of these activities relinquished.

na tatsiddhau loka-vyavaharo heya kintu phala-tyagas tat-sadhanam ca karyam eva

na-not; *tat*-that (free from anxiety); *siddhau*-in the perfection; *loka*-worldly, mundane; *vyavaharah*-interactions with; *heya*-to be given up; *kintu*-rather; *phala*-of the results; *tyagas*-renounced; *tat*-that; *sadhanam*-means of development; *ca*-and; *karyam*-obligations; *eva*-indeed

We are advised to continue our presence in the world, taking care of our family, going to work, and so on. Only a fully ripe bhakti might abandon convention. Until then we try to offer every action to the Beloved. The world offers so many spiritual opportunities. As an example, if someone is rude to us we can gauge how much progress we are making by the degree and intensity of our reaction. If someone is suffering, we can console. We abandon any expectation of reward or rebound. Amma says we should be a giver not a taker. Most people in this world are takers and see every action, every relationship is a means of satisfying one or more desires or needs.

> It is more blessed to give than to receive. *Bible, Acts 20:35*

186

Sutra 63 – Worldliness should be avoided

Stories about sex, riches and the travails of worldly people should be avoided.

Stri-dhana-nastika-caritram na sravaniyam

Stri-of women (here 'sex'); *dhana*-wealth; *nastika*-and nonbelievers, worldly people; *caritram*-stories; *na*-not; *sravaniyam*-listened to

These things are all great distractions. They pull our mind outward to the senses when we should be focusing our mind inward on our Beloved. We have long standing habits of imagining we are going to derive pleasure from these things and so we listen with rapt attention as the spider webs are spun.

Further, listening to these stories will entice us to indulge in them. Doing so encourages us to continue our fantasies regarding the attainment of happiness from the world. This also applies to watching movies that revolve around these distractions.

A comment from Yogananda:

> It is extremely important to conserve your power of sex. Overindulgence in sex and misuse of Nature's creative force will bring on disease and old age quicker than anything else. It devitalizes the body and weakens the immune system. Married couples

should practice moderation, and single persons should observe abstinence. Yogananda 2000:14

And another comment by Amma:

> Those who are overly attached to sports, games and movies should not keep the television in their room. The temptation will be too much for them to resist. During the period of sadhana (spiritual practice) it is best to keep away from circumstances which will arouse one's passions.

> Do you know why the opposite sex becomes an enemy, spiritually speaking? When our parents had sexual intercourse, they never had a desire to have a virtuous and brilliant child. It is the same samskara (tendency) that is lying in us. Weren't we born from the same blood? The thought that lies in one's mind is that the opposite sex is only for one's pleasure. In order to remove this vasana (mental habit), one should keep one's distance, while perceiving them in a brotherly or sisterly way. Amma, *Awaken Children*, vol. 1

> Again I tell you, it is easier for a camel to go through the eye of a needle than for someone who is rich to enter the kingdom of God. Jesus, *Matthew*, 19:24

Sutra 64 – Abandon egoism, pride and negativity

Egoism, pride and other negative mental afflictions should be abandoned.

abhimana dambah- adikam tyajyam

abhimana-pride; *dambah*-deceit; *adikam*-and so forth; *tyajyam*-should be given up

The ego is the opposite of love. Pride is a manifestation of ego along with other negative afflictions such as jealousy, anger, greed, lust and attachment. Pride is perhaps the most insidious of these because it can be so very subtle. We don't see it coming. By comparison, the other afflictions are easily seen. For example, anger is obvious.

Ego is destroyed by love so the practice of spiritual devotion will be of great benefit in this regard. At the same time that we are cultivating love, we should be weeding out the afflictive emotions. In order to do this, we have to be able to see them and most people are not able to admit they have these afflictions because there is a deep seated fear that somehow we are not OK; we are a loser – a failure; we are deficient; we are ashamed and guilty; we are a miserable wretched sinner; there is a good reason one of our parents didn't like us – and so on. Often these feelings, that something is lacking, are subtle and hard to see because they have become so thoroughly ingrained in our psyche and our perception. Therefore, step number one is learning to accept ourselves just as we are.

We are not talking about loving ourselves as that is most likely going to be a form of self-cherishing or ego. If we love ourselves, as in have attachment, we will still not be able to fearlessly and objectively look at our faults because the faults will conflict with our conjured "lovable" projection of our self. For example, the mind will refuse to see pride because it conflicts with our perception of being lovable. If a person has true unconditional love for themselves, they will also have it for everyone else. For most this is not the kind of love we will have. If we can accept ourselves – the good, the bad and the ugly - then we will be able to observe our afflictions. When we observe our afflictions, we can talk to the Beloved about it and offer them to Her.

Amma comments:

> Without God's Grace, we cannot see Him. If we want to get His Grace, the ego in us should go. The well might say, "Everyone is drinking water from me. If I am not here, how will they cook food?". But the well does not know that it was dug by someone and that the bricks which make it beautiful were made by somebody else. Our situation is also the same. We become egotistical thinking that "I am greater than everything else". But even to move a finger we need God's power. (Pointing Her finger at a distance) However powerful a cyclone is, it cannot do anything to that blade of grass. Whereas the huge trees standing with their heads high will be uprooted. All grace will flow to us if a servant-like

attitude (dasa bhavana or attitude of humility) comes to us. After that, nothing can move us. But God will not abide where there is ego. We will be uprooted by the cyclone of ego.   Amma, *Awaken Children*, vol. 1

And Krishna

Those who are free from pride and delusion, who have conquered the evil of attachment, who are constantly dwelling in the Supreme Being with all lust completely stilled, who are free from dualities of pleasure and pain; such wise ones reach My Supreme Abode. Krishna, *Bhagavad Gita*, 15.05

Sutra 65 – Place all actions on God

If these passions cannot be controlled, direct them to God – place all your actions on God.

tad arpitakhilarcarah san kama-krodhabhimanadikam tasminn eva karaniyam

tat-to the Beloved; *arpita*-having offered; *akhila*-all; *acarah*-actions; *san*-being; *kama*-selfish desire; *krodha*-anger; *abhimana*-pride; *adikam*-and so forth; *tasmin*-toward the Beloved; *eva*-only; *karaniyam*-should be done

When we perform actions and give them to the Lord, our mind will be purified even if one or more of the afflictive emotions are present. For example, we may have resentment for someone who has given us a task but if we give the task to our Beloved, realizing the task was given to us by the Beloved, the resentment will be dissipated. Anger is a difficult emotion to manage because we go temporarily insane when we become angry. We are not able to think, "The Lord caused all this to happen and so what is there to be angry about?" When the madness of anger comes upon us, there is no reasoning about anything.

In every instance that we give these actions and our negative emotions to God there will be a painful resistance. This is known as *tapas* which literally means heat. If we are on a diet and desire some food that is forbidden, and we say "no," we feel an uncomfortable heat or tension.

Amma comments:

> Children, if you want to fight, you should fight against God. That will make you reach the goal. If you fight with humans, you will become evil like them. Your life will be wasted, everything will be lost, and both parties will be destroyed. If you seek help, seek God's help. Arjuna fought with the help of Krishna and won. Duryodhana fought with the help of soldiers, and although he had much wealth, the result was complete destruction. Therefore, live with complete surrender to God. You can tell your sorrows to God. If you want to quarrel, you can quarrel with God. Children, you should develop this kind of mental attitude.   Amma, *Awaken Children*, vol. 2

The following comment by Amma is more about how to surrender to God and not so much about sublimating our afflictive emotions. However, the advice is so profound and so clear that it was not possible to resist posting it here:

> Amma: Concentration and love are one, like two sides of a coin. Love should be there if you want concentration. It is impossible to make them stand separately. They are inseparable, just as the length and breadth of an object are inseparable.
>
> When we have love for something, an incessant and unbroken stream of thought flows towards that object. The thoughts are only about that. Therefore,

to really love we need concentration and to really concentrate we need to love the object, whatever it may be. One cannot exist without the other. A scientist who does experiments in the laboratory needs a lot of concentration. Where does this concentration come from? From his deep and intense interest in that subject. From where comes this deep interest? It is the result of intense love that one has towards his particular subject or field of study. Conversely, if one concentrates on a subject intensely, love for it will also develop.

It is experienced that there is tastelessness behind taste. What makes us feel this taste and tastelessness? These impressions are created by our own actions. We feel them because of the vasanas (mental tendencies) inherited from our father and forefathers. We forsake the quest for permanent spiritual bliss as we pursue worldly pleasures. Having abandoned sweet pudding, we go after crow droppings. Remembrance of God and repetition of the mantra is necessary in order to escape from this bondage to worldly pleasures. As we walk we should try to chant our mantra once with each step, repeating it over and over again, step by step. Thus while walking, we can remember God as we chant His Holy Name.

You should repeat your mantra even while lying down. Embracing the pillow, you should imagine that it is God. You should have the strong faith and conviction that God is always with you and will certainly appear before you if you call with longing. Try not to commit any mistakes and try not to get angry with anyone. Immediately when you get up in the morning, you should think of God and pray, "O Mind, you should only turn towards the right path. Travel towards God's world. Do not go towards the empirical plane."

The Holy Mother continued,

Amma: Children, you should develop an attitude of bowing down to anything and everything. Keep the plate of food in front of you and bow down to the food before eating and bow down to the plate after eating. An attitude to prostrate to anything at any time should come. In this way, an awareness, "for what am I doing this," will arise. Thus we should build up good character. Prostrate to the cloth you will wear. Bow down to the water with which you will take a shower. During these occasions of bowing down, you will have a pure resolve to see the same consciousness in everything whether with form or without. While doing so, you are in fact remembering God. While taking a shower, imagine that you are doing so with the Lord. Even if you are on the toilet, imagine that you are talking to Him. Do not waste any time. Simply do it. Constant remembrance of God, irrespective of time and place, is real devotion. If you practice in this manner, He will come; He must come. God will come and play with you. Imagine that you are talking to Him while performing any action, whatever it is. Amma, *Awaken Children*, vol. 3

THE BEACHCOMBER

Mother of Life
I am so happy to spend my days
  roaming at the ocean's edge
    of your infinite being
  listening to the rolling surf
    as it calls the sparkling star filled sands
      to join the timeless push and pull
        of your ecstatic play

I am a beachcomber, a vagabond
  looking for a few good sea shells
Soon we will take these to the market place
  hoping that someone else
    might hold a shell to their ear
      and hear your song
        of endless love

[From the author's book *Soft Moon Shining*]

Sutra 66 – Love is the only reason for existence

Going beyond the three forms (tamas, rajas, sattva) of devotion, the devotee sees himself as God's eternal servant or eternal bride and one's only reason for existence is to love.

Trirupabhangapurvakam nityadasyanityakantabhajanatmakam prema karyam premaiva karyam

Trirupa – three forms; *bhanga* – breaking away; *purvakam* – previously (mentioned); *nitya* – eternal; *dasya* – devoted servant; *nitya* – eternal; *kanta* – wife; *bhajana* – worship; *atmakam* – the nature of (one's only reason); *prema* – love; *karyam* – duties; *premaiva* – love only; *karyam* - duties

The intellect can never go here. In fact, love is not only the reason for our own existence, but also for the entire universe. Having transcended the three *gunas* (forms – tamas, rajas and sattva), the lover has no "reasons" left. Reasons are the children of these forms, as discussed previously, and each of these forms imposes qualities on our devotion. Now there is only love. Nothing else. This is quite beyond the mind. The devotee lives in love, lives for love and lives as love. Even when the ego has been completely consumed, the devotee will retain a small bit of it in order to continue loving the Beloved. After Nisargadatta Maharaj attained perfect spontaneity (merging in the Self), he continued to worship a picture of his deceased guru three times a day until the time that Nisargadatta left his body.

Kabir has these words:

> O Sadhu! The simple union is the best.
> Since the day when I met with my Lord,
> there had been no end to the sport of our love.
> I shut not my eyes, I close not my ears,
> I do not mortify my body;
> I see Him with eyes open and smile,
> and behold his beauty everywhere;
> I utter His name, and whatever I see,
> it reminds me of Him; whatever I do,
> it becomes His worship.
> The rising and setting are one to me;
> all contradictions are solved.
> Wherever I go, I move round Him,
> All I achieve is in His service.
> When I lie down, I lie prostrate at His feet,
> I am immersed in that one great bliss
> which transcends all pleasure and pain

[Kabir, *Songs of Kabir*, translated by Rabindranath Tagore, published by Samuel Weiser, 1977]

Sutra 67 – Given themselves solely to God

Devotees who have given themselves solely to God are the highest.

bhakta ekantino mukhyah

bhakta-lover of God; *ekantinah*-single-minded; *mukhyah*-foremost, primary

As a result of reading this sutra, it is not clear whether Narada means single-minded bhaktas are the highest of all spiritual practitioners – or – among bhaktas, those who have given themselves solely to God are the highest. The answer is found in sutra 25 in which Narada proclaims that the path of bhakti is superior to all other paths. Therefore, the single-minded bhakta is the highest among all spiritual practitioners. Highest means they are the most direct and their realization is the most complete because it includes both form and the formless.

Krishna comments on the simplest, safest, most beautiful, most blissful and easiest of all paths:

> And I consider the yogi-devotee — who lovingly contemplates on Me with supreme faith, and whose mind is ever absorbed in Me — to be the best of all the yogis. Krishna, *Bhagavad Gita*, 6.47

> Arjuna asked: Those ever steadfast devotees who worship the personal aspect of God with form(s),

199

and others who worship the impersonal aspect, or the formless Absolute; which of these has the best knowledge of yoga?

Lord Krishna said: Those ever steadfast devotees who worship with supreme faith by fixing their mind on a personal form of God, I consider them to be the best yogis.

But those who worship the unchangeable, the inexplicable, the invisible, the omnipresent, the inconceivable, the unchanging, the immovable, and the formless impersonal aspect of God; restraining all the senses, even-minded under all circumstances, engaged in the welfare of all creatures, also attain God. Krishna, *Bhagavad Gita*, 12.01-04

Paul echoes the idea that the practitioner of love is of the highest order:

If I speak in the tongues of men and of angels, but have not love, I am only a resounding gong or a clanging cymbal. If I have the gift of prophecy and can fathom all mysteries and all knowledge, and if I have a faith that can move mountains, but have not love, I am nothing. If I give all I possess to the poor and surrender my body to the flames, but have not love, I gain nothing. *1 Corinthians 13:1-3 NIV*

Sutra 68 – They are permeated with God

When such speak of God, their voices stick in their throats, they cry and weep, their hairs stand on end; and it is they who give holy places their holiness; they make good works, good books better, because they are permeated with God.

kanthavarodharomancasrubhih parasparam lapamanah pavayanti kulani prthivim ca

kantha-of the throat; *avarodha*-with blockage, choking; *romanca*-with bodily hair (standing erect); *asrubhih*-tearfully; *parasparam*-with one another; *lapamanah*-talking; *pavayanti*-they purify; *kulani*-communities; *prthivim*-the earth; *ca*-and

This sutra gives a clear indication of the symptoms of one who is divinely intoxicated and reveling in the ocean of endless bliss. Ramakrishna concurs:

> Brahmo devotee: What is the sign of one who has attained true wisdom living in the world?
>
> Ramakrishna: When the repetition of the Name of the Lord will bring tears to the eyes, send a thrill through the whole body and make the hair stand on end. The spiritual eye must be opened. It is open when the mind is purified. Then the presence of Divinity will be realized everywhere and every

woman will appear as Divine Mother. *Gospel of Ramakrishna*, translated by Swami Abhedananda

And rapture with Amma:

A group of devotees who had come from the northern part of Kerala started singing verses from the Devi Mahatmyam:

O Devi (God as the Divine Mother; God in the feminine form), You who remove the sufferings of Your supplicants, be gracious. Be propitious, O Mother of the world. Be gracious, O Mother of the universe. Protect the universe. You are, O Devi, the ruler of all that is moving and unmoving.

You are the sole substratum of the world, because You subsist in the form of the earth. By You, who exist in the form of water, all this (universe) is gratified. O Devi of inviolable valor.

You are the power of Vishnu, and have endless valor. You are the primeval Maya, which is the source of the universe; by You all this (universe) has been thrown into an illusion, O Devi. If You become gracious, You become the cause of final emancipation in this world.

All lore are Your aspects, O Devi; so are all women in the world, endowed with various attributes. By You alone, the Mother, this world is filled. What praise can there be for You who are of the nature of primary and secondary expression regarding (objects) worthy of praise?

There was so much love and devotion in their melodious chanting of the Sanskrit slokas that some of them became very absorbed. Lost in their own world of ecstasy, they began displaying different gestures—stretching out their arms toward Amma, raising them high, joining the palms of their hands and saluting Amma. Some shed tears of love as they continued singing the chant with tremendous devotion. The devotees were thrilled at the chance to sing for Amma. As Amma sat looking at them, compassion flowed from Her eyes. Her face shone like the full moon. Amma's mere glance with the bewitching smile She wore on Her lips threw a spell of quivering enchantment over the devotees. Tears rolled down their cheeks as they soared to heights of supreme devotion while they continued to chant the hymn.

Amma sat very still on the cot. She manifested all the signs which She expresses during Devi Bhava— Her hands held in a divine mudra, a blissful smile radiating from Her face—as She gazed at the devotees who were chanting. A tidal wave of supreme devotion arose in them as their singing became more ecstatic and the entire hut vibrated to its fullness. She sat in that mood for some time, then

She turned away from them but remained in an indrawn state. The chant slowly subsided. Perfect silence prevailed in the darshan hut. The devotees experienced the bliss of deep meditation. One of the devotees was in a totally intoxicated mood. With a heart filled with devotion and love, he cried and laughed at the same time as he called out 'Amma... Amma' every now and then. Some of the devotees sat fixing their gaze on the Holy Mother's face. Nearly five minutes passed in this way before Amma slowly opened Her eyes chanting Shiva... Shiva... Shiva... Shiva... while moving Her right hand in circles, a familiar but inexplicable gesture to the devotees.   Swami Amritaswarupananda, *Awaken Children*, vol. 5

Sutra 69 – They make everything holy and sacred

They add holiness to holy places, nobleness to acts and they elevate mere writings to the level of sacred scriptures.

tirthi-kurvanti tirthani su-karmi-kurvanti karmani sac-chastri-kurvanti sastrani

tirthi-into holy places; *kurvanti*-they make; *tirthani*-sacred places; *su-karmi*-into auspicious works; *kurvanti*-they make; *karmani*-acts; *sac-chastri-kurvanti*-foundation for authority; *sastrani*-sacred scriptures

A God realized soul is firmly fixed in Truth. It is not strong belief or faith but absolute knowing. This is the source of their power – their divinity. Everything that comes into their field of being is blessed and transformed. They are like a magnifying glass that is passed over the world. Everything caught in the gaze of the magnification is irrevocably changed whether we are aware of it or not. This is why it is so very important that we never pass up the opportunity to sit in the physical presence of a God realized soul. This is thoroughly discussed in sutra 39 and well worth reading multiple times. Maya will be the cause of forgetting about this.

> As She was talking, the Mother (Amma) entered into 'bhava samadhi'. After some time chanting 'Siva...Siva...Siva', She became Her normal self. The Mother continued,

205

Mother: Wherever Jivanmuktas (God realized souls) go, the people will go after them. They don't have to look nor do they have to search for disciples. People will go on following them. People will be attracted to them even without their knowledge just like rubbish caught in a whirlwind. That is the power of a person who does sadhana. Either their breath or the wind that blows over their body is enough to benefit the world.   Amma, *Awaken Children*, vol. 1

LOTUS FLOWERS

Mother of life
The minds of your children
Are lotus flowers
Floating on your lake of fire
Rooted in the soil
Of primordial awareness

Your wind dancers
Visit us often
And there is much joy
Passed among us
Sharing the cup
Of the seasons
Watching the reeds of time
Being split
Into blades of laughing love

[From the author's book *Divine Mother of the Universe*]

Sutra 70 – They are given the fullness of God

They are given the fullness of God to know the presence of the Beloved in and around themselves at all times.

tanmayah

tat-that, those bhaktas; *mayah*-God's fullness

> M: "When one sees God does one see Him with these eyes?"
>
> Master: "God cannot be these physical eyes. In the course of spiritual discipline one gets a 'love body', endowed with 'love eyes', 'love ears', and so on. One sees God with those 'love eyes'. One hears the voice of God with those 'love ears'. One even gets a sexual organ made of love."
>
> At these words M. burst out laughing. The Master continued, unannoyed, "With this 'love body' the soul communes with God. Ramakrishna, *Gospel of Ramakrishna*, p. 115, translated by Swami Nikhilananda

Sri Ramakrishna is telling us that we can connect with God and communicate with God directly by developing a "love body." This connection and communion is even more intimate and direct than talking to our spouses or best friends. In the beginning we may feel little or no connection to God. As the practice of devotion develops and expands, this conduit of communion begins to form between God and ourselves. We discover a long sealed hatchway in our psyche that we begin to slowly dismantle thus allowing love to flow from God to us in ever-increasing measures. As this connection develops, we experience feelings of intense bliss, ecstatic joyous weeping, intoxicated laughter, and deep communion.

As our connection expands in frequency and intensity, a subtlety of mind or sensitivity develops. This increased sensitivity, along with inexplicable waves of ecstatic love, will lead us to the direct knowledge that these experiences are actually and definitely God returning our love. It will seem as though we had been chipping a hole from the inside of our prison wall of the ego and God had been chipping a hole from the outside and then we breakthrough. We continue chipping away through devotional practice and the hole enlarges. At last it is large enough for us to touch fingers with God. Tears will come easily and frequently. We will say God's name and have tears. Soon, the hole becomes large enough for us to step through and embrace God completely and be embraced by God – personally and directly. We will begin to experience God's love spontaneously and in strange places such as the grocery store checkout line. When we experience God's love in this way it is more than simply God throwing blessings on us. It is as direct and personal as if we were talking to another human being. We know we are talking and walking with God and we know God is also directly aware of us.

Eventually, the specific form of God we had chosen to worship becomes the universe and all of its beings as a whole. Oddly, this expansive way of relating to our Beloved becomes the most intimate.

[The preceding text is from the author's book *Finding God's Love*, www.devipress.com – a how-to book for the practice of spiritual devotion].

Amma comments on knowing God:

> Question: Is it possible to know God for those of us who are ordinary people?
>
> Mother: Children, God is also ordinary at all times and therefore not difficult to know. But there is one thing. The ignorant ones who are drowning themselves in worldliness cannot know the Truth. Whoever it may be, he who has sincere interest can know and see God.

WAITS AT THE EDGE

Our Beloved has made a careful web
Spun with strands of bliss
It waits at the edge of darkness
Where every sorrow
Melts into joy
And where every soul that is caught
Cries out with overflowing
Roaring rivers of love filled joy
So loudly and so sweetly
And with so much love
That the entire universe hears it
And every being and every creature
Is filled with endless love

Sutra 71 – Forefathers rejoice and the gods dance

When a man loves God so much, his ancestors rejoice, the gods dance, and the earth gets a Master!

modante pitaro nrtyanti devatah sa-natha ceyam bhur bhavati

modante-become joyful; *pitarah*-forefathers, ancestors; *nrtyanti*-dance; *devatah*-demgods; *sa-natha*-endowed with a master; *ca*-and; *iyam*-this; *bhuh*-the earth; *bhavati*-becomes

Scriptures say that when a person becomes liberated (from the ego a.k.a. enlightened) that the ancestors will be greatly benefited for a number of generations backward and also forward. It is something akin to throwing a rock in a pond and the waves of beneficence travel into the past and the future.

The gods and angels dance because a shining light has been born into the universe interpenetrating all levels of consciousness and all beings are benefited. The gods dance in ecstasy to experience such a lover of God living in the world. In the midst of material darkness, a great light is now shining.

In this way the earth gets a true teacher and Master.

Sutra 72 – No differences to such lovers

To such lovers there is no difference of caste, sex, knowledge, form, birth, or wealth.

nasti tesu jati-vidya-rupa-kula-dhana-kriyadi-bhedah

na asti-there is not, irrelevant; *tesu*-in them; *jati*-of class; *vidya*-education; *rupa*-beauty; *kula*-family; *dhana*-wealth; *kriya*-occupation; *adi*-and so on; *bhedah*-difference

Because the lover sees the Beloved in all forms of the material universe, no substantial difference can exist from person to person. God is the light of ten million suns (that means an infinite number of suns ☺) shining from the very core of every human being, every creature, plant and atom. Everyone and everything is made of "God stuff." The lover sees this clearly and so shallow differences are no more than the differences seen in snowflakes. Every snowflake is made of the same substance.

From the author's book *Finding God's Love*:

> How can it be that there are seemingly so many individual beings yet all of them have their existence in the same I AM? This is God's slight-of-hand. The universe and all of us in it are holographic. In other words, each part contains the sum of the whole. The following prayer from the Hindu Vedas reveals this mystery.

That is the Whole, this is the Whole;
From the Whole, the Whole arises;
Taking away the Whole from the Whole,
The Whole remains.

Yajur Veda, Brhadaranyaka Upanishad, 5.1

A holographic picture has a unique property. If we take a pair of scissors and cut the picture into ten pieces, we will have ten whole and complete reproductions of the one original. As another analogy, we can say that each person and each creature is like a spoke on a wheel with God as the hub. At every moment God is the very life which supports us and *is* us. Take away the hub and there is no wheel and there are no spokes. In yet another analogy we can liken each individual to a lens on the eye of a fly which has hundreds of individual pictures but only one observer behind it. God is the observer and each individual being is a lens on the eye. Or we can say that each individual mind is a mirror and one mind looking at another is like two mirrors opposing each other which creates the appearance of limitless images trailing off into infinity. In reality there is only one being and one God appearing as "the many." God is like an endless fountain that bubbles up from the center of our being as light, life and love. For most of us the awareness of this is very dim and obscure. What Jesus taught was rediscovering this wellspring of eternal life.

Jesus answered, "Everyone who drinks this water [ordinary well water] will be thirsty again, but whoever drinks the water I give him will never thirst. Indeed, the water I give him will become in him a spring of water welling up to eternal life." *John 4:13-14, NIV* (brackets by author)

Sutra 73 – For they all belong to God

For they all belong to God.

yatastadiyah

yatah-since; *tadiyah*-belong to him (God)

Not only do they all belong to God but everything we own or have including our bodies belongs to God. Any spiritual insight we may have garnered was given to us solely by the grace of God. There is absolutely nothing we can call our own except the ego and it is an illusion!

Ramakrishna:

> Rama Chandra (the God Incarnate) once asked his great devotee Hanuman: "My son, in what relation do you regard me?" The devotee replied: "When I think of myself as embodied, I am Thy servant and Thou art the Lord. When I think of myself as the Jiva (Ego) I am Thy part and Thou art the Universal Whole; but when I think of myself as the Atman, I am one with Thee. Then I realize 'I am Thou and Thou art I.'"

> If the sense of "I" clings to one so persistently, let it remain like that of a true Bhakta who thinks of himself as the servant of the Lord.

> "I" and "mine" — these two are the signs of *Ajnanam*, ignorance. My house, my wealth, my learning, my

glory, all these are mine — this idea proceeds from ignorance of one's true Self, but *Jnanam* or divine knowledge means that state where Jiva realizes: "O Lord, Thou art the Master of all; house, family, children, friends, relatives, nay, whatever exists in the universe belongs to Thee." "Whatever is mine is Thine." "Nothing belongs to me" — such ideas rise from true knowledge.

It is good for everyone to remember that after death nothing of this world will remain with us.

Gospel of Ramakrishna, translated by Swami Abhedananda

Sutra 74 – Logic and intellectual grasping

Logic and intellectual grasping are to be avoided.

vado navalambyah

vadah-speech as intellectual discourses; *na*-not;
avalambyah-relied upon

The use of logic to explain or illuminate love by the use of thoughts and concepts is ill advised. There may be some conceptualizing regarding love, but this will be having to do with how we may find love and not love itself. For example, we may discuss backpacks, ropes and carabiners that will be used to ascend Mt. Everest but any discussion as to the breathtaking beauty seen from the peak is futile.

Intellectual grasping is the nature of any intellect. It wants to put love in a definable box and be able to say the box is so high by so wide by so long. This is the habitual nature of the intellect. When it fails to do this, it denies that there is such a thing as love – that is pure, selfless, unconditional love.

In our Western culture, we are brought up thinking the intellect is God and that it will solve all of our problems, provide security and entertain us. Because of this, very few of us arrive at adulthood with a heart. Thus, there is no love and no compassion. The progression of this heartless, mechanistic, self-centered view is what Pope Francis called the *Globalization of Indifference*.

217

Sutra 75 – Can never fathom the unfathomable

Because these can never fathom the unfathomable, they continue endlessly and to no good end.

bahulya-avakasatvad aniyatatvat ca

bahulya-excessive, extensive; *avakasatvat*-space; *aniyatatvat*-lacking clarity; *ca*-and

A sincere spiritual aspirant will feel like a failure if someone calls him or her an intellectual. The intellect is useful for certain things in the empirical world but it is mostly useless in spiritual matters.

Too much dependence on the intellect will always result in doubt. The end game of the intellect is to declare that what can be perceived by the five senses is all that is real and all else is fantasy. In truth, the reverse is true. That which is known by the heart is rock-solid real and everlasting while that which is known by the senses is temporary – fleeting – impermanent; like clouds in the wind.

The intellect that is allowed to have its way is often going to be an atheist.

This is perhaps the most distressing disability of the intellect. It is not able to accept a thoughtful, loving God; that the entire universe is the body of a conscious, willful, architect that has love for us and is interested in our well-being; that the sum total of existence is a cosmic person – a cosmic mind. For this reason, intellectuals will feel more comfortable on the path of jnana yoga or raja yoga both of which are in pursuit of the impersonal Self. Understanding the Beloved as the personal aspect of the infinite is the last step in Adi Shankara's three-part axiom.

1. The world is an illusion
2. Brahman is real
3. Brahman is the world

Brahman is the formless substratum of existence. Many who pursue the Self by self-enquiry fail to realize the third step which gives Brahman form – makes God personal. They will insist the that there is nothing real about the universe and that it is a dream to be ignored – nothing more than a projection of the mind. This view arises because the third aspect of Shankara's axiom has not been groked. Form, the universe, is eternal according Shankara who is regarded as the father of modern non-dual (jnana) philosophy. He was also a great devotee of the Divine Mother which is commonly overlooked by practitioners of the jnana yoga path. The reader is invited to explore the last chapter in this book which was included to clarify the practice of jnana yoga (advaita, non-duality, Vedanta).

For the practice of bhakti (spiritual devotion), the intellect should be checked in and boarded at a nearby kennel while you are exploring the vast space of love.

THE AUTUMN LEAF PILE

Sweet Mother of life
The best thing about this mind
   is that it can ask
      why anything exists at all!

And then become stupefied and awestruck
   at having fallen
      into the absolute and unanswerable

Like a child that spins in dizzying circles
   to discover that walking in a straight line
      or even walking at all
         vanishes in the thrill
         of such an altered state of being

Sweetest Mother
What fun it is to dive head first
   into the autumn leaf pile
      of your many mysteries
         that you have so carefully raked
         over this vast stretch of endless time

[From the author's book *Soft Moon Shining*]

Sutra 76 – Devotional books and practices

One should read books that are flush with devotion and one should do practices that increase it.

bhakti-sastrani mananiyana tad-bodhaka-karmani karaniyani

bhakti-spiritual devotion; *sastrani*-holy scriptures; *mananiyana*-reflected upon; *tat*-that (spiritual devotion); *bodhaka*-made known, awakening; *karmani*-actions' spiritual practices; *karaniyani*-performed

The point here is to immerse oneself in devotion. There is so much great devotional poetry – Rumi, Kabir, Hafiz, Ramprasad. Singing devotional songs (hymns, bhajans, kirtan) and playing them on the stereo or in the car.

The author's book *Finding God's Love* is a how-to book on the practice of spiritual devotion and contains much information on meditations and visualizations to cultivate the flame of love. You can review the book and/or purchase it at www.devipress.com.

221

Sutra 77 – Renounce attachments and work hard

Giving up all desires of pleasure and pain, gain and loss, worship God day and night. Not a moment is to be spent in vain.

sukhaduhkhecchalabhadi tyakte kale pratiksamane
ksanardhamapi vyartham na neyam

sukha-happiness; *duhkha*-sadness,suffering; *iccha*-selfish desires; *labha*-worldly gain; *adi*-and so on (other personal concerns); *tyakte*-having given up; *kale*-time; *pratiksamane*-always enthusiastic; *ksanardhamapi*-fraction of an instant; *vyartham*-uselessly; *na*-not; *neyam*-should be spent

We are in a dream of our own creation that we have overlaid onto the cosmic dream. Our own interpretation of reality if you will. It is a dream of desires that can never be satisfied. It is a dream of relentless fears biting at our heals like a pack of ravenous wolves. Both of these miseries keep us running but we have the lead weights of laziness and ignorance on our feet. Samsara (endless cycles of births and deaths) consumes us again and again like so much flesh in a meat grinder. We are consigned to suffer and it has been this way for so long we think the nightmare is normal.

There is a purpose to the suffering and that is to encourage us to wake up and do something about it. But we don't understand it. As we get older, we see more clearly that life in this world is suffering as the Buddha revealed in the first of his *Four Noble Truths.*

The book *Rama's Most Excellent Dispassion – The Path to Bliss* is for exploring the possibility of waking up, renouncing our attachments and finding the path to bliss. The book is by the author of this book and can be reviewed and/or purchased at www.devipress.com.

> "Meaningless! Meaningless!" says the Teacher. "Utterly meaningless! Everything is meaningless." What do people gain from all their labors at which they toil under the sun? *Ecclesiastes 1:1*

Amma comments:

> You children should live with the remembrance of God. Do not waste time. Repeat your mantra while doing each action. Practice meditation every day for some time.

> Student: Mother, how should we practice meditation?

> Mother: Place a small picture of a God or Goddess that you like in front of you. Sit gazing at the picture for some time. Then try to fix the form within while closing your eyes. Again look at the external picture when the form within fades away. Again the eyes should be closed. Imagine that you are talking to the Beloved Deity, "Mother, do not go away

abandoning me. Come into my heart. Let me always see Your beautiful form" and so on. Cry, embracing your Beloved Deity. That which we meditate on will appear in front of us if constantly repeated like this with faith.

A COUNTRY FAIR FOR THOSE MAD WITH LOVE

Drive me out of my mind, O Mother!
What use is esoteric knowledge
   or philosophical discrimination?
Transport me totally with the burning wine
   of your all-embracing love.

Mother of Mystery, who imbues with mystery
   the hearts of those who love you,
   immerse me irretrievably
   in the stormy ocean without boundary,
   pure love, pure love, pure love.

Wherever your lovers reside
   appears like a madhouse
   to common perception.
Some are laughing with your freedom,
   others weep tears of your tenderness,
   still others dance, whirling with your bliss.

Even your devoted Gautama, Moses,
   Krishna, Jesus, Nanak, and Muhammad
   are lost in the rapture of pure love.

This poet stammers,
   overcome with longing:
"When? When? When?
When will I be granted companionship
   with her intense lovers?"
Their holy company is heavenly,
   a country fair for those mad with love
   where every distinction
   between master and disciple
      disappears.

This lover of love sings:
Mother! Mother! Mother!
Who can fathom your mystery,
   your eternal play of love with love?

You are divine madness, O Goddess,
   your love the brilliant crown of madness.
Please make this poor poet madly wealthy
   with the infinite treasure of your love."

[*Mother of the Universe*, poems of Ramprasad, translated
by Lex Hixon, published by Quest Books.]

Sutra 78 – Non-violence, compassion, purity

Ahimsa (non-violence), truthfulness, purity, compassion, and godliness are always to be kept.

ahimsa-satya-sauca-dayastikyadi-canitryani paripalaniyani

ahimsa-non-violence; *satya*-truthfulness; *adi*-and so forth; *sauca*-purity, cleanliness; *daya*-compassion; *astikyadi*-faith in spititual teachings; *canitryani*-the characteristics; *paripalaniyani*-should be cultivated

Everything and every being and every person is now the Beloved. An act of violence toward any person or Nature is an act of violence toward God. Being untruthful is a delusional negation of everything being God. Whatever comes our way we should accept personally. This does not mean we refrain from acting on the behalf of others in a compassionate way. Purity is innocence.

> The childlike innocence deep within you is God. Amma, *Awaken Children,* vol. 6

> And he said: I tell you the truth, unless you change and become like little children, you will never enter the kingdom of heaven. Jesus, *Matthew 18:3*

Wisdom is knowing we are all one; love is what it feels like and compassion is what it acts like. We now feel the pain of the suffering of others because they are our Beloved.

Our love for the Beloved and thus love for others causes the fires of compassion to burn.

The more our attention is focused on our Beloved the more we become like Him/Her. As a man thinketh so is he (goes for women too). Qualities such as humility, patience, forbearance, kindness and cheerfulness begin to radiate from our person and this is godliness.

> Be ye therefore perfect, even as your Father which is in heaven is perfect. Jesus, *Matthew* 5:48, KJV

Sutra 79 – Unceasing worship

The Lord alone should be worshipped at all times, with all one's heart and soul, and with a calm mind.

sarvada sarvabhavena niscintaih Bhagavaneva bhajaniyah

sarvada-at all times; *sarvabhavena*-in every way; *niscintaih*-anxiety free; *Bhagavan*-God; *eva*-only; *bhajaniyah*-to be worshiped

This sutra reminds us of Jesus' first commandment (we will show both of his two commandments here):

> One of the teachers of the law came and heard them debating. Noticing that Jesus had given them a good answer, he asked him, "Of all the commandments, which is the most important?" "The most important one," answered Jesus, "is this: 'Hear, O Israel, the Lord our God, the Lord is one. Love the Lord your God with all your heart and with all your soul and with all your mind and with all your strength.' The second is this: 'Love your neighbor as yourself.' There is no commandment greater than these." [The teacher/man replies]: "Well said, teacher," the man replied. "You are right in saying that God is one and there is no other but him. To love him with all your heart, with all your understanding and with all your strength, and to love your neighbor as yourself is more important than all burnt offerings and sacrifices." When Jesus saw that he had answered

wisely, he said to him, "You are not far from the kingdom of God." And from then on no one dared ask him any more questions. *Mark 12:28-34, NIV*

And my tongue shall declare Your righteousness And Your praise all day long. *Psalm 35:28*

HAPPY TO CONTINUE

Beloved Mother of the universe
Your children
Are happy to continue
To endure the suffering
Of individual existence
So we can continue
To love you

The thought of you
Being alone
Is more sadness
Than we can bear

Sutra 80 – Thus worshipped day and night

Giving up all other thoughts, the whole mind should day and night worship God. Thus being worshipped day and night, He reveals Himself and makes His worshippers feel Him.

sa kirtyamanah sighramevavirbhavatyanubhavayati bhaktan

sa-he, God; *kirtyamanah*-worshipped, sincerely venerated; *sighram*-hurriedly; *eva*-indeed; *avirbhavati*-comes into being; *anubhavayati*-gives realization; *bhaktan*-to the devotees

It sounds radical to say that we should give up all other thoughts. Yet that is precisely what is needed and it can be done. This is accomplished by making the mind one-pointed or directed at one thing – in this case the Beloved.

For the bhakta, the path to this is keeping the mind on the Beloved even while working. Amma recounted the story of a fisherman in a narrow canoe standing and performing many actions. All the while he never lost concentration on his balance. This was explained in Sutra 36.

The author met an Amma devotee, an older woman, who is able to say her mantra without losing concentration non-stop regardless of activities. She said that she began by saying the mantra all through her meals. Then expanded from there.

We would like to repeat this Amma quote:

In order to realize the Atman, the mind has to dissolve. As long as there is a mind, you will be dominated by the ego.

People point their finger at insane people and call them 'crazy.' But they don't know that they themselves are actually crazy, as well. Whoever has a mind is mad, because the mind is madness. In the case of a person who is insane, it is clearly manifested and therefore you can see it. Whereas, in your case, it is not so clearly manifested and therefore not as obvious. But the madness is there, because the mind is there.

By "mind" Amma means that which identifies with everything, constructs opinions, harbors fear and rides bareback on the bouncing broncs of desire. She doesn't mean the faculty of speech or the ability to add numbers.

It is the mind that embellishes our experience with memories and interpretations. It's the mind that imagines fantasies and makes things up convincing us that it is real. It's the mind which prevents us from experiencing life directly. It's the mind that is so restless and noisy that we can't feel the subtle energies of love and aliveness that fill the sacred space of every moment lived.

By fixing the mind on the Beloved, two things occur. The mind becomes still and God answers our call. The mind, now being still, can then fully hear God's response and feel His love.

Sutra 81 – Love alone is the highest reality

In all of the past, present and future, love alone is the highest reality!

trisatyasya bhaktireva gariyasi bhaktireva gariyasi

trisatyasya-in the triune reality; *bhaktih*-devotion to the Beloved; *eva*-alone; *gariyasi*-is most significant

Perhaps this is the best of all the sutras. There is very little love in our world. We are born with love because it is our innate nature but the world beats it out of us. Our goal is to rediscover this love.

And let's not forget that, according to the Bible, *1 John 4:8*, God is love!

There are only two ways to approach what is real. The first is the Self. This is pure, empty awareness - the ocean in which the universe floats. The second is love. This is pure, empty being - the ocean in which the universe floats. It is not possible to have awareness without love nor is it possible to have love without awareness. They are really inseparable. The Self (awareness) is Brahman and love is Shakti (primordial energy).

The Self does not feel like anything. It has no qualities – no characteristics. One can't experience it because one *is* IT. But one can realize that one is the Self. It is the mind that comes to know this and not the Self. It is the mind that realizes it is the Self. It is the mind that becomes enlightened and not the Self. The Self can't know anything because it is changeless. Thus there are no occurrences in the nature of Brahman. But it is what grants knowing due to its eternally static nature. There is an eternally occurring contrast between the eternally changeless Self and eternally changing Shakti.

When the mind merges in the Self, there is the feeling of love, aliveness, being and bliss - satchitananda. In one sense the mind and the universe (Shakti) are totally dependent on the Self (awareness). In another sense, the Self is totally dependent on Shakti (mind et al). The Self (awareness) is inconsequential and meaningless without Shakti. They are really an inseparable whole.

We can't say that Brahman or the Self is a reality. It is not any-thing that is other than awareness. However, we can say that love is reality and that it is the highest reality from which every other form of "reality" is manifested. Love is the gold that makes all the jewelry that forms the universe. Love is Shakti the primordial energy of existence. Shakti is regarded as being feminine – the Divine Mother of all.

WHO ARE YOU?

Beloved Mother
Who can understand
Your mysterious being?
Having come from nowhere
You have woven
Brightly colored clothes
For the pure formless Absolute
And with the joy of a small girl
You thoughtfully dress him
For each occasion
In just the right way

You have given him eyes of light
So he could see his reflection
In the clear lake
Of your innocent smile
And you have passed
The plate of sacraments
To all of your children
So that he could love
And be loved

Mother
Your unfathomable being
Is like a well with no bottom
That yet overflows
With dreams and visions
And creatures and plants
All born

In the flashing lightning
Of your touch

Mother just who are you?
The Absolute is nothing
Without you!
Before your magnificent love
He was a homeless beggar
Clothed only in empty space

[From the author's book, *Divine Mother of the Universe*,
www.devipress.com]

Sutra 82 – Eleven basic modes of devotion

Though devotion itself is a singularity, it manifests in eleven basic modes.

gunamahatmyasakti-rupasakti-pujasakti
smaranasakti-dasyasakti-sakhyasakti
vatsalyasakti-kantasakti-atmanivedanasakti
tanmayatsakti-paramavirahasakti-rupa
ekadha api ekadasadha bhavati

gunamahatmyasakti-embracing the Lord's qualities; *rupasakti*-embracing the spiritual forms; *pujasakti*-embracing ceremonial worship; *smaranasakti*-embracing continuous remembrance; *dasyasakti*-embracing service; *sakhyasakti*-embracing as a dear friend; *vatsalyasakti*-embracing with the affection of a parent; *kantasakti*-embracing as a loving wife; *atmanivedanasakti*-embracing the knowledge of the Self; *tanmayatsakti*-embracing attitude of oneness; *paramavirahasakti*-cherishing the supreme separation; *rupa*-form; *ekadha*-singular; *api*-though; *ekadasadha*-of eleven; *bhavati*-becomes manifest

Contemplating the greatness of God
Cherishing God's beauty and form
Loving to worship God
Remembering God at all times
Being the servant of God
Being the friend of God
Being an affectionate parent to God
Being married to God

Dedication to God
Becoming absorbed in God
Permanent self-obliteration in God

BOWING IN THE WINDS

Mother of silence
What enchanting beauty
   you harbor on the shining brow
   of time and space

What joy can be greater
   than having an eye to drink it
   or an ear to touch it?

Mother I am a blade of grass
   bowing in the winds
      as your galloping riders
      of creation and dissolution
         sweep the universe
            allowing not a single spec
            to escape the bliss
               of your radiant light

Everywhere we look there is only you!
   Dancing in the ebb and flow
   of eternal being

[From the author's book *Soft Moon Shining*]

Sutra 83 – Great sages on the path of devotion

Thus the luminaries of the path of devotion - Sanatkumara, Vyasa, Suka, Sandilya, Garga, Vishnu, Kaundinya, Sesha, Uddhava, Aaruni, Bali, Hanuman, Vibhishana and others-proclaim unanimously without fear of the criticism of men.

ityevam vadanti janajalpanirbhayah ekamatah Kumara-Vyasa-SukaSsandilya-Garga-Visnu-Kaudinya-Sesa-Uddhava-Aruni-Bali-Hanuman-Vibhisana adayo bhaktyacaryah

ityevam-in this way; *vadanti*-they proclaim; *janajalpah*-common opinion; *nirbhayah*-without fear; *ekamatah*-of one voice; the Kumaras, Vyasa, Suka, Sandilya, Garga, Vishnu, Kaundinya, Sesha, Uddhava, Aaruni, Bali, Hanuman, Vibhishana (the champions and proponents of spiritual devotion); *adayo*-and others; *bhakti*-spiritual devotion; *acarya*-founding exemplars, authorities

Narada introduces us to other great sages who have taught and illumined the path of spiritual devotion.

Sutra 84 – With faith we can realize the Beloved

Those who believe and have faith in this auspicious teaching given by Narada, become blessed with devotion and will realize the Beloved and attain the Beloved. Yes, that one obtains the Dearest Beloved!

ya idam Narada-proktam sivanusasanam visvasiti sraddhate sa bhaktiman bhavati sa prestham labhate sa prestham labhata iti

ya-whosoever; *idam*-this; *Narada-proktam*-spoken, revealed by Narada; *sivanusasanam*-divinely auspicious instruction; *visvasiti*-has full faith, belief; *sraddhate*-is convinced by; *sah*-that one; *bhaktiman*-endowed with devotion; *bhavati*-becomes; *sah*-that one; *prestham*-the Beloved; *labhate*-attains; *sah*-that one; *prestham*- the Dearest Beloved; *labhata*-attains; *iti*-thus

Amma comments:

Remove the darkness of ignorance by thinking of God with a burning heart. There should be total surrender to that One within in the form of one's own soul. Know that if the Compassionate One is pleased, your life will be fulfilled. For those who take refuge in Him with sincere devotion, God is for them Eternal Bliss Itself.

Jnana - Advaita – Non-duality

An Appendix

The following is a discussion about misconceptions and pitfalls in the practice of the path of jnana. The author spent a number of years practicing and studying this path prior to meeting Amma which is recounted in the author's autobiographical book *Into the Mystic* which can be reviewed at www.devipress.com. This discussion is included in this book to clarify misconceptions regarding the practice of jnana because it is discussed a number of times by Narada. Some might see jnana and bhakti as competing paths but they are not. Both end in the same place. Amma says jnana is the end, bhakti is the means. Jnana, though simple in concept, is very difficult to practice. Bhakti is the easiest, safest and most direct path to the Infinite.

The author considers that it might be better if the teachings of jnana (a.k.a. advaita, Vedanta, non-duality) were kept secret and only given to persons who are of sufficient maturity. This view is bolstered and appreciated by the author's own deluded period when he was thinking he was enlightened as a result of certain non-dual experiences and from reading the teachings of Ramana Maharshi and Nisargadatta Maharaj (this period of "enlightenment" is thoroughly illustrated in the author's book *Into the Mystic*). Unless the practitioner is of sufficient maturity and has a Self-realized satguru as a guide, the practice of non-duality is likely to make one lazy and crazy.

Nisargadatta Maharaj in the book *I Am That* underscores the central problem:

"There are so many who take the dawn for the noon, a momentary experience for full realisation and destroy even the little they gain by excess of pride. Humility and silence are essential for a sadhaka, however advanced. Only a fully ripened jnani can allow himself complete spontaneity."

A person reads the books and has an experience. He or she then concludes they are enlightened and it's all over with. Never mind the contradiction of their actions which play out as anger, frustration, fear and upsetedness. The author once made the mistake of pointing this out to a person on FaceBook who claimed to be enlightened causing the enlightenee to reply with a choice word of vulgar origin and informing the author as to what he could do with it.

The pseudo-enlightened person rationalizes that these emotions are simply the One-Self that is expressing the infinite play of existence. The newly enlightened person never asks why there is anger if there is only One-Self. Who is there to be angry with whom? Why is there frustration if all is my own Self? The same is true for fear. Ramana was once asked how to know a Self-realized person and he replied we know them by their utter lack of fear. Once a person succumbs to the pitfall of thinking they are enlightened, it is almost impossible to coax them out of it. It is very difficult for someone to wake up who is dreaming that they are awake.

The newbie has a moment of non-duality but, due to the fact that they are not spiritually mature, the ego returns and claims the experience. It says, "I am enlightened. I had an experience." In the experience there was no "I" but it returns now with full force and, in fact, the ego swells. It is now enlightened. The ego now imagines itself to be special and above the rest of humanity who have not yet become special (enlightened). Pride takes the ball and races for the end zone of endless delusion.

The effect of this is to make us crazier than we were prior to the experience. We then see the manifestation of all sorts of perversions of non-duality. The author refers to persons manifesting these perverted points of view to be suffering from "non-dual disease." Here are a few of the symptoms:

1. No guru or teacher is necessary because our own Self will teach us. Antidote: Understand that we end up taking lessons from the deluded mind not the Self. Whether learning carpentry or brain surgery, a teacher is required. Why not spirituality? For most of us, we have no awareness of the Self because it is obscured by the mind. All we know are our fears and desires. An outer guru is necessary to awaken us to the guru within and guide us around the pitfalls.

2. We should not do any spiritual practice because that is a denial of the truth that we already are the Self. Antidote: We must make an effort to reach the effortless state. The ego is not real but simply saying so will not get rid of it.

3. It's all a dream; nothing is real. Antidote: For a Master it's a dream but for us everything is quite real. Try to stop eating or sleeping to see if you are a Master. Pull your fingernails out and see if you can smile complacently while repeating, "It's all a dream."

4. Love and compassion are unreal products of the mind. Antidote: This is how the intellect sees it because the intellect can't go there. Love and compassion are all that's real.

The internet is full of people saying such things. Listening to them, the author sometimes feels he is hearing the cacophony of the dayroom in an insane asylum.

The most unfortunate aspect of having wandered into the false assumption that we are enlightened, is that we become closed to any further progress. We actually are worse off than before "enlightenment" and the door is slammed shut. We believe we now know everything there is to know and we are not open to any other suggestions. This is indeed most unfortunate and it is the main reason why it might be better if these teachings were not circulated among the unprepared.

The ironic truth is that if someone says they are enlightened it is a sure sign they are not. Here is a nice quote from Papaji regarding this:

"If you see the illusion you are enlightened but if you think you are enlightened, you are in the illusion."

And another good one from Amma from the book *From Amma's Heart*:

"Questioner: Amma, do you claim anything?

Amma: Claim what?

Q: That you are an incarnation of the Divine Mother or a fully Self-realized Master and so forth.

A: Does the president or prime minister of any country keep on announcing, "Do you know who I am? I am the president/prime minister," wherever he or she goes? No. They are what they are. Even to claim that you are an Avatar or are Self-realized involves ego. In fact, if somebody claims that they are an Incarnation, a Perfect Soul, that in itself is proof they are not.

Perfect Masters have no such claims. They always set an example to the world by being humble. Remember, Self-realization doesn't make you special. It makes you humble.

In order to claim that you are something, you neither have to be Self-realized nor do you need any special skill. The only thing that you need is a big ego, false pride.   That is what a Perfect Master doesn't have."

Do we see this clearly? If a person is truly enlightened, it means they no longer have a sense of "I" or any identification with being an individual person. If that is true, then who is there left to be enlightened? There is no "I" that can claim to be enlightened. There is no "I" left that can say, "I had an enlightenment experience." The phrase, "I am enlightened" is an oxymoron.

Most persons who claim to be enlightened and who are giving talks and writing books are still deluded. It is not difficult to read books on non-duality and then repeat it like a parrot and fool most people. They may even have had a non-duality experience or two which only makes things worse.   However, most of them are themselves fooled because they have put new wine in old bottles meaning their minds were not pure and so the experience has been made putrid by the ego.   Non-dual disease follows.   They may really imagine themselves to be enlightened or awake or partially awake.

A few of these may have advanced stages of awakening but they are not satgurus. A satguru is one who has merged in the Self completely.   They function from a completely spontaneous realm as indicated in the previous quote from Nisargadatta regarding "perfect spontaneity." They have no desire to accumulate followers and so they make no claims. They teach only as an act of compassion. They are fearless. They do not experience anger or frustration. If they appear to express anger it is only to get the attention of a student who did not get the message the first few times when it was expressed in a passive tone. These beings are very rare.

Even with the case of avatars or incarnations of the Divine, there will be a period of intense spiritual practice. This was true for Ramakrishna, Yogananda, Amma, Ramana Maharshi and Nisargadatta. For example, Ramana had his initial enlightenment then sat in meditation absorbed in the Self for three years. He sat 24/7 and did not speak for three years. He referred to this as a period of purification. The author interprets "purification" to mean the destruction and dissolution of the ego. If someone claims to be an enlightened teacher, we should look for this kind of intense spiritual practice in their past. Imagine – Ramana sat twenty-four hours a day, every day for three years and didn't speak the whole time! We need to see this kind of intensity. A person claiming to have had an enlightenment experience one day out of the blue while walking in the park is most likely still packing an ego.

What would constitute spiritual maturity sufficient to begin the practice of Self-enquiry? Are there any prerequisites? Those persons suffering from non-dual disease will claim that Advaita does not have prerequisites and that anyone, anywhere can take up the practice. This is really a very difficult practice! Yes, the concept is very simple and intellectually gratifying but doing it is very difficult. About this Amma says:

"Those who reach the Goal through the path of jnana can be counted on the fingers of your hand." Amma, *Eternal Wisdom*, vol. II, p. 124

Sri Ramakrishna said:

"To know God through jnana and reasoning is extremely difficult." Ramakrishna, *The Gospel of Ramakrishna*, p. 94

Those who propose this path say things like, "All you have to do is be yourself. Just let go and be the Self." The title of one popular book containing quotes from Ramana is *Be As You Are*. The problem with this is that we are currently imagining ourselves to be a collection of memories, desires and fears that reside in our minds. This is what we think we are. Simply saying, "Be as you are" is misleading. It sounds easy but getting rid of the memories, desires and fears is most difficult. Until our habitual identification with these is burnt to a crisp, we will not be able to be the Self. We will only know our dreams and these will continue to create more desires and more fears which will constantly be snapping at our heels like a mad dog.

This path, as with all paths, requires much effort. Remember Ramana sitting 24/7 for three years? It all depends on our "earnestness" as Nisargadatta was fond of saying. It is difficult to coax the mind into remaining in the state of self-enquiry which is meditating on or contemplating the source of the "I." It is very dry and unrewarding up until the final dissolution. There are a few exceptions with Ramana being one. He had a spontaneous awakening when he was sixteen (which culminated in the three year period he called "purification"). This occurred because he was already Self-realized from previous births. Very rarely does this happen. Nisargadatta Maharaj comments on this in *I Am That*:

"Q: But can a Guru give realisation without words, without trust, just like this, without any preparation?

M: Yes, one can, but where is the taker? You see, I was so attuned to my Guru, so completely trusting him. There was so little of resistance in me, that it all happened easily and quickly. But not everybody is so fortunate. Laziness and restlessness often stand in the way and until they are seen and removed, the progress is slow. All those who have realised on the spot, by mere touch, look or thought, have been ripe for it. But such are very few. The majority needs some time for ripening. Sadhana (spiritual practice) is accelerated ripening.

Q: What makes one ripe? What is the ripening factor?

M: Earnestness of course, one must be really anxious."

It should be noted that Nisargadatta left his family, and spent all day, every day concentrating on Self-inquiry for four years. Then he attained permanent realization. It is said the floor cracked where he was pacing back and forth due to the intensity of his concentration. He was deeply absorbed all day, every day.

Bhakti, or the path of devotion and love, is an easier path because one begins to get the bliss right away. God invites his lovers directly into the living room of the heart. Also the practice of bhakti is not nearly as prone to the pitfall of pride. Jnanis, or practitioners of Advaita / non-duality, must wait until the very end to experience the bliss of the Self. This is why it is so difficult to maintain the earnestness and intensity practicing non-duality. Few can do it. Thus Amma says the number of people who will achieve the goal with this path can be counted on one hand.

Advaita should only be practiced in the presence of a fully Self-realized satguru. This guru should possess the yogic power of being able read all of our thoughts. If the practitioner succumbs to pride or becomes a victim of non-dual disease, the guru will be able to make corrections.

Advaita Prerequisites

In the *Advaita Bodha Deepika*, it says Advaita should only be taught to those...

> "...who are fitted (by all) their sins (adharmic actions) having been burnt off by austerities practiced in several past births, their minds made pure, their intellects discriminating the real from the unreal, themselves indifferent to the pleasures of either this or the other worlds, their minds and senses under control, passions held down, actions given up as a worthless burden, faith firm and minds tranquil, eagerly seeking release from bondage."

In these modern times, there are many people who believe that there are no prerequisites for Self-enquiry. They believe Advaita can be pursued by anyone, in any circumstance and that their life-style and background has no relevance. They reason, using their intellect, that Advaita is a simple concept of abiding in our true Self which is ever present in all persons. Why should that be prefaced by requirements?

This idea of no requirements and the afore mentioned perversions of non-duality, are often referred to as neo-Advaita philosophy. Among the teachers of this line of thinking, the idea of conditions or prerequisites is rarely discussed. We are told that we can practice non-duality within the context of an affluent, hedonistic lifestyle and that little or no modification of our behavior or mental tendencies is required. Of course this is very convenient and therefore appealing. This attracts followers, fills lecture halls and retreats with high-paying customers and sells books. Few would show up if they were told the truth.

However, if we look at classic texts on Advaita, we see a much different story. The necessity of "fitness" on the part of the student is a fundamental topic discussed at the beginning of the teaching. The requirements are not for those lacking in courage or commitment. They are daunting to say the least.

First of all, the applicant should renounce the world, be celibate, and become adept at other yogas such as Raja Yoga, Karma Yoga and Bhakti Yoga. One can read texts such as the *Vedanta Sara I.6-26* for greater illumination of this subject.

We can probably assume few were ever in possession of one hundred percent of these requirements. It will nonetheless promote humility for both the student and the teacher who may himself be short on some of the requirements!

Ramana summarizes all of this by stating simply that one must have a "ripe" mind to pursue Advaita. This is the sum of the essence of it all. It sounds simple but, upon closer examination, we may find that the condition of having a ripe mind is quite elusive. A ripe mind is not easy to come by and few have one. Nisargadatta also mentions in his quote a few pages back, that for most people "ripening" is needed and for this he recommends doing spiritual practices.

In Ramana's own words, a ripe mind possesses deep detachment and profound discrimination. At the top of the list in order of importance is a powerful longing to be liberated from the body and Samsara (the seemingly endless cycles of birth, death and rebirth). This is not a shallow mental fascination but rather an irrevocable conviction that runs deeply into the very root of our feelings and thoughts. Detachment and discrimination themselves will open a universe of discovery should one undertake a study of these prerequisites. It will then become clear just how "unripe" our minds actually are. We can read more about this in *Ramana Gita* VII 8-11.

A ripe mind is a sattvic mind. Sattvic means a state of peaceful and harmonious equilibrium. Sattva is one of the three states of existence which are needed to compose the universe. The other two states are "rajas" and "tamas." These are the qualities of passion/activity and ignorance/inertia respectively. To have a ripe mind, the qualities of rajas and tamas must be diminished in the mind and also the body so that sattva predominates. Vedic thought sees the body and mind as connected so the sattvic condition is necessary for the body as well. Otherwise the mind will have difficulty being sattvic. In our current times, we can see that our culture is dominated by rajas and tamas.

To arrive at a sattvic or ripe mind, it is necessary to practice a dharmic life-style. This is like the prescription of the "do's" and "do not's" of the yamas and niyamas which are prerequisites for the practice of Yoga. Regarding this, Ramana especially recommended a vegetarian diet which is sattvic and therefore beneficial to acquiring a ripe mind. Alcohol is very tamasic and should be avoided.

The basic problem with neo-Advaita practice is that most people take Ramana's "ripe mind" in a shallow, self-serving way. No one wants to sacrifice anything or feel the heat of tapas (denial of desires). No one wants to change their mental attitudes or their behavior. No one wants to challenge their pride or their anger or stop being judgmental of others. Few want to be vegetarian. Everyone wants Advaita but nobody wants to give up anything. As a result, the concept of "ripe mind" is put on the shelf as no more than a quaint aphorism to which one need not pay much attention.

Not Far Enough

It is the author's opinion that most practitioners of Advaita do not go far enough.

The Indian philosopher and spiritual Master Adi Shankara (circa 800 CE) is widely regarded as the father of modern non-dual philosophy. Curiously, he was an ardent devotee of the Divine in the form of the Divine Mother. He wrote many beautiful hymns and poems of adoration to her. Most neo-Advaitans would not consider worshipping the Divine in any form believing as they do that all form is unreal and only the formless is real. This is because they have not developed far enough in their insight. Sankara's three point axiom illustrates this.

1.   The world is an illusion
2.   Brahman (God) is real
3.   Brahman is the world

Most practitioners of the path of Advaita are stuck at step one or two. Remember, according to Amma, the number of people in the entire world who can realize the end game of complete and irrevocable absorption in the Self / God by the path of Advaita can be counted on the fingers of one hand.

Few non-dual practitioners will ever realize that Brahmin is the world. However, Shankara did and this explains his deep undivided devotion to an all-pervasive cosmic being he called the Divine Mother. He states in his book *The Crest*

Jewel of Discrimination, that form or Maya is eternal. It was not created. It will not cease to be. It just simply always has been and always will be. This eternal status of the universe is further underscored in the Vedas which explain that the universe comes into being, expands, then contracts and is dissolved. Then the cycle repeats again and for all eternity it does this. The Self or Brahman is eternally unchanging while the universe is eternally changing. Such a pair they are! There is no beginning or end to either and they are really one whole.

The result of step three is that we realize and understand the entire universe(s) to be a single, conscious being who expresses intelligence, design and will. Not only that but it will communicate with us, talk to us, love us and accept our love. Call it what one will – Adi Shankara liked to call it the Divine Mother. Thus devotion is not only the simplest, and the safest but also the highest form of spiritual practice.

> Mother showed the tip of one of Her fingers. "In front of bhakti (devotion for God), mukti (liberation from the cycle of birth and death) is no more than this." Amma, *Eternal Wisdom*, book 2

> The state that we attain by calling and crying to God is equal to the bliss that the yogi experiences in Samadhi. Amma – *Awaken Children* book 3

OTHER BOOKS BY THE AUTHOR

Read about or purchase any of the author's books:

www.devipress.com

INTO THE MYSTIC

A Story of Light, Love and Bodacious Spiritual Adventures

In 1967 at the age of nineteen, Ethan was unsuspectingly catapulted from his self-imposed, fortress of atheism to swimming in the ocean of the Divine in one blinding, mind-melting flash of insight. He never looked back. This is the story of a lifetime of spiritual pursuit. From hippies and the cultural revolution to the Rosicrucians to the I Am School to the Summit Lighthouse to Self-inquiry (non-duality) to love and devotion – bhakti - with priceless guidance from his guru Amma beginning in 1988. This is one man's journey, spanning more than fifty years, through the brambles and the thickets; through the ancient halls of mystery, the pure emptiness of being and into the bliss of the Divine Light. This is a story of love, love and more love; a transfiguration from mind to Heart.

THE MYSTIC CHRIST

The Light of Non-duality and the Path of Love According to the Life and Teachings of Jesus

The Mystic Christ is an ancient tale of mystic union, salvation, and enlightenment. It is the careful uncovering of a lost treasure of immeasurable value, long buried in the suffocating darkness of conventional orthodoxy on one side, and blind fundamentalist extremism on the other. From the viewpoint of the world's mystical religious traditions, the brilliant light of the Master's way is revealed as a penetrating radical non-duality unifying all people and all of life. His path to this all-embracing unity is the spiritual practice of pure selfless love. Love God intensely, love our neighbor as our own Self, bless those that curse us, and pray for those that mistreat us. Love has been lost, becoming nothing more than a word in the dictionary and, yet, it remains the foundation of Jesus' message.

The Mystic Christ is also a compelling story of the ego, the personification of ignorance, and how it has distorted and subverted the sublime sayings of the Master, twisting reality into unreality and light into darkness. The ego is the Antichrist in this ancient drama that has gripped every culture for all time in its talons of self-centered perception. The ego is anti-love.

Adam and Eve were not the first people, the nature of man is good, scripture is not infallible, Jesus is one of the ways, all religions are paths to God, reincarnation is in the Bible,

257

the resurrection as a personal spiritual awakening, and the error of eternal damnation are all carefully and lovingly revealed in the life and sayings of Jesus.

The Mystic Christ is thoroughly punctuated with quotes from Buddha, Krishna, Lao Tzu and other masters of the mystical traditions. But, most importantly, over 230 scriptural references from the Old and New Testament are used to illustrate the harmony that exists between the life and teachings of Jesus and the world's great religions.

With the skill of a surgeon, the author removes 2000 years of ego-centered bindings that have hidden the brilliant light of the Master from the world. *The Mystic Christ* is at once profoundly fascinating, deeply historic and electric with the vibration of the mystical experience. Review or purchase at www.devipress.com.

108 HUGS FOR JESUS

The Ecstasy of Divine Love as a Path to God

The deepest longing of every soul is to experience the Divine directly, personally and intimately. To have this direct communion is the purpose of our human birth and nothing else in all of eternity will ever satisfy us or truly make us happy. The path to this is hidden and Jesus said few will find it. It is not something that can be found in any church or any book as it must be searched for and discovered in the Heart. At the center of our being, there is a doorway to God's infinite light, love and bliss. It is here, within us, that God waits for us – calling for us – yearning for our love. The kingdom of God is truly within us - Luke 17:21. This book is a comprehensive guide to this greatest of all human endeavors - the Divine Romance; the lover and the Beloved; the eternal Companion.

Jesus prescribed a path to this ecstatic union with His two commandments – love your God with all your heart, mind, soul and strength and love your neighbor as your own self. In Luke 10:25, Jesus says practicing these two commandments is all that is necessary to attain eternal life. In this book, is a thorough discussion of the practice of Jesus' commandments including theory, history, techniques and pitfalls. Love is what every soul needs more than anything else. Love is what is most needed in the world. Divine Love and how to become that love is the primary focus of this book.

As an aid to practicing Jesus' first commandment to love God, a collection of 108 phrases describing key aspects of the Lord's teachings and life events has been provided with commentary. Chanting these with love and devotion is one way that we can increase the fire of our love for the Beloved. There is nothing in all of eternity that is sweeter, more magnificent, more illuminating, more liberating, more healing or more blissful than spiritual love for the Divine. So take off your clothes, empty your mind and step into the ocean of God's infinite love! Review or purchase at www.devipress.com.

FINDING GOD'S LOVE

The Theory and Practice of Love and Devotion as a Spiritual Path

Love is the primal essence. Love is the light of the Divine which fills the vastness of eternity with the sweet fragrance of immortal bliss. The practice of love and devotion is an ancient path leading to direct mystical experience of the Supreme. Notable teachers of this path include Jesus, Hafiz, Narada, Ramprasad, and Amma (Mata Amritanandamayi). *Finding God's Love* is suitable for any pilgrim of any faith who wishes to experience a direct and personal communion with the Divine. God's lovers will find immediate access to the living room of God's heart where they will revel in the bliss and joy of the universe; divinely intoxicated in the breath of the eternally radiant now; swept away in an endless celebration of life.

The first part of the book reveals how love works to release the human psyche from the fetters of its own self-imposed limitations. Love is the antidote to all negative emotions. Love heals the festering wounds that lay buried in our past. Love cleans the lens of the soul allowing the light of the Divine to percolate up from the center of our being illuminating our personal world. The second part of the book explains the practical aspects of this path including meditations, visualizations and prayer. The last section is a collection of teachings from Amma, the hugging saint, on the practice of love and devotion.

Love is what makes life beautiful because God *is* love. Love nourishes the delicate flowering of the immortal soul vanquishing boredom once and for all in the magnificence of its ever-fresh ever-mysterious river of divine grace. This book is an invitation to ecstasy - to swim in the ocean of God. Review or purchase at www.devipress.com.

RAMA'S MOST EXCELLENT DISPASSION

The Path to Bliss

Over 5,000 years ago, Rama, the God Man / avatar, walked the earth to restore truth and dharma. As a young boy not yet 16 years old, he ponders the nature of the world. Pulling back the curtain of Maya, exposing the underbelly of the psychosis of human kind, he is astonished to find that we are living in a dream world wholly divorced from reality. In the opening pages of the classic Hindu spiritual text *Yoga Vasistha*, he explains his disillusionment and his dispassion toward worldly existence to his father and his guru Sri Vasistha. He does this with astonishing force and poetic beauty. This book, *Rama's Most Excellent Dispassion*, presents Rama's oration and follows with an exploration of the meaning and scope of Rama's disillusionment. Rama's dispassion is both radical and blissful. It is the agony and the ecstasy. It is a precious opportunity for and light. the reader to unfold spiritually and swim in the ocean of love. Review or purchase at www.devipress.com.

WHOLE FOODS PLANT BASED DIET

**Save the Earth, Save your Health,
Save the Animals**

The greatest single repository of evil on the planet today is the eating of farmed animal products. It is destroying our planet, destroying our health and causing intense suffering for billions of farmed animals. 90 percent of the clearing of the rainforest in South America is for the raising of beef cattle. Farmed animals produce more greenhouse gas than all modes of human transportation combined. The practice is very wasteful and inefficient as It takes eleven pounds of grain to make one pound of beef. Animal agriculture consumes more fresh water by far than all human consumption combined. And this is only the tip of the iceberg. According to the United Nations and the World Health Organization, we will need to stop the practice of animal agriculture if the human race is to survive. The seriousness of this cannot be understated. The practice of raising livestock for human consumption is wholly unsustainable.

Most people are not aware of the horrific suffering animals endure at the hands of profit motivated meat and dairy producing enterprises. Animals endure this suffering and have been enslaved by human kind for only one reason and that is to satisfy our taste buds. This is the worst of all possible reasons to ask an animal to suffer and to slaughtered at a very young age.

Numerous comprehensive scientific studies such as the China Study, have proven beyond all doubt that eating animal flesh and dairy products is very detrimental to our health causing, cancer, heart attacks, strokes, diabetes and many more debilitating diseases.

Read this booklet and watch the videos *Forks Over Knives*, *Cowspiracy* and *Earthlings*. Do some research and then change to a plant-based, whole-foods cuisine. Save the earth, save your health and save the animals! Do it now before it's too late! Review or purchase at www.devipress.com.

A PILGRIM'S GUIDE TO AMMA

A Field Handbook for Entering and Exploring the World of Mata Amritanandamayi

Mata Amritanandamayi, commonly known as Amma, is a mysterious and supremely powerful river of unconditional love. Having never taken even a single breath for herself, she has come to this world only to give. The rest of us, as seekers, as children of light, have a very rare opportunity in being able to have access to such a Divine phenomenon. If we are suffering she gives comfort. If we are intent on the Divine, she gives instruction and direct experience. She is always giving with a tremendous outpouring of love and compassion that is a wonder to behold.

Amma asks nothing in return. We can keep our religion or current path if we like. We are not asked to sign up for anything. Amma will help is with whatever spiritual endeavor we may have undertaken – no strings attached. Amma says her religion is love.

Amma's "largeness" is beyond understanding but what we can see is profoundly astonishing. It is the purpose of this book to give a brief view of Amma's life, accomplishments and her uplifting impact on people just like us. We will have to look far and wide in the scrolls of human history to find a Divine manifestation that has done as much for humanity, is as powerful as Amma and, at the same time, so supremely accessible to anyone and everyone.

In the past 40 years Amma has tirelessly hugged over 34 million people. Why would anyone do this and do it for free? This alone speaks to the fact that Amma is a Divine person extraordinarily endowed with the ocean of Divine Shakti (power) and limitless love. Her charities for the poor and the suffering are vast. It boggle's the mind to consider that all this was done by a short, cute Indian lady, born into a very poor family who never made it past the fourth grade. Dear reader, you are invited to step into this book and see what Amma has to offer you. Review or purchase at www.devipress.com.

SOFT MOON SHINING

Poems for the Mother of the Universe

Soft Moon Shining is an invitation to step into the heart of the Divine Mother. Her perpetual dance of cosmic bliss plays out through the eons as the creation and dissolution of worlds within worlds. Yet God, in the feminine form of the Mother – as the Absolute made Immanent – is ready to shower Her love and affection on any who care to turn their gaze toward Her fiery heart.

This work of poetry is both profound and beautiful in its ability to arrest the reader's conventional mind plunging the soul into the cauldron of divine intoxication and bliss. Each poem is a meditation on the Mother of the universe. Feel Her love and Her compassion as the Divine Mother hugs each reader in an embrace of timeless love.

Dance with god in the form of the Mother! Revel in the call of the infinite! Swoon with joy as the heart opens wide to the roaring river of Mother love. Purchase at www.devipress.com.

SOFT MOON SHINING

My beloved Divine Mother
Dance with me
     under the soft moon shining
     in the wide open fields
        far beyond the toil and trouble
        of my busy mind

Dance with me
  before the night grows old
     while the winds of love
     still bow the grasses
        and the coyotes cry for you
        to step their way

Dance with me my beloved
  while the Mystery's Edge
    still flirts in the shadow
    of your radiant light

DIVINE MOTHER OF THE UNIVERSE

This Is How We Love You

Poetic meditations on the Divine Mother published in 2015.

TOUCHED THE OTHER SIDE

Mother of the universe
You have conjured
This dancing ocean
Of earth and plants
And beings and stars
From your dark womb
Of formless mysteries

And you hold
The crackling thunder
Of emptiness
In your begging bowl
Of endless time

And it is you who writes
Poems of love
In letters of molten gold
In the deepest cave
Of our hearts

Your children weep with joy
At your slightest touch
Flooding the world

267

With the brilliant lightning
Of awareness

That it was always you
Behind the curtains
Of coming and going

Your children are bowing
So low to you Mother
That our faces
Have touched
The other side

Read about or order books: www.devipress.com

Made in the USA
Charleston, SC
01 October 2016